Sport Parachuting

The author in his element

Sport Parachuting

Charles Shea-Simonds

Second Edition

Adam & Charles Black
London

FIRST PUBLISHED 1971
SECOND EDITION PUBLISHED 1975
BY A. & C. BLACK LIMITED
4, 5 & 6 SOHO SQUARE, WIV 6AD

© 1971, 1975 CHARLES SHEA-SIMONDS

ISBN 0 7136 1574 5

Printed in Great Britain by
REDWOOD BURN LIMITED
Trowbridge & Esher

CONTENTS

Section I—Learning to Parachute

Section II—Further Parachuting Progression

ILLUSTRATIONS

Dedicated to the memories of
Ray Etchell and Les Woolgar,
both true sport parachutists.

FOREWORD

The need for an up-to-date, comprehensive and practical book of instruction on sport parachuting has been with us for a number of years. It has now been met by one of the most experienced and respected members of the growing number of British sport parachutists. Everyone with an interest in the sport will have cause for satisfaction, and I hope that "Sport Parachuting" will be read widely by experts and novices alike.

Charles Shea-Simonds would probably be among the first to admit that compared to other recognised sports, parachuting is still almost in its infancy. We may expect to see changes in attitude, technique, standards, and above all equipment in the years to come. There is probably more scope for new ideas, refinements and improvements in the outlook of this pastime than any other which calls for similar qualities. For this reason his valuable book will never, in this edition, be accepted as the definitive work on the sport. I look forward to seeing further revised editions at intervals, as new ideas and equipment take shape.

To those who have recently taken up sport parachuting or are contemplating doing so, I would only offer two thoughts. The first is that parachuting is not normally a dangerous business. It is only likely to become so as a result of someone doing something foolish. This is a pity because foolishness is avoidable. It therefore behoves everyone as in skiing, motoring, flying and similar activities, to recognise the value of good instruction based on wide experience and sound judgement. In this respect Charles Shea-Simonds and others like him have much more to offer newcomers in addition to writing about the sport.

Lastly, whether we look at free-fall parachuting as it is today or as we visualise it might be in years to come, we are still likely to recognise that it is, and will remain two sports combined in one. Even among experienced exponents of the art there are differing views on the attractions and challenges connected with that part of a long delayed-opening jump which precedes the deployment of the parachute, and that part which follows it; when the parachute becomes not only vitally necessary but an instrument which responds to the most delicate handling. Each of these totally different sensations has its own charm, so often and so inadequately described by many who have fallen victims to the spell of this sport which has no equal. If this book succeeds in bringing these joys to some who otherwise might never experience them it will be judged to have been successful on this score alone.

15 March 1971   Major-General R D Wilson CBE, MC

PREFACE

The public at large generally equate parachuting with stocky, crew-cut, combat-scarred troops jumping into battle, fairly bristling with weapons or with pilots abandoning flaming aircraft and taking to the silk. But parachuting can be a sport within the strictest definition of the word: 'a pastime of an outdoor or athletic kind'. It is about the sport of parachuting that I write. It is a new and exhilarating sport which has grown within the last twenty years to attract dedicated participation by people of both sexes and from all walks of life.

This book is not a history of parachuting, although that in itself is fascinating enough from the story of the first ever parachute descent by a certain Andre Jacques Garnerin over Paris on October 22, 1797, to Leslie Irvin's historic first ever free fall on April 28, 1919 over McCook Field, Ohio, and the Frenchman Leo Valentin's discovery of free fall body control in 1948. Nor is it a collection of reminiscences of hair-raising parachuting exploits. It is designed as a handbook for the newcomer to the sport of parachuting and he should read it in conjunction with what he learns from his instructor. To this end I hope it will be of benefit.

I am extremely grateful to Major-General Dare Wilson for writing the foreword to this book; it was as Chairman of the British Parachute Association that he did so much to have parachuting recognised officially as a sport in this country, and the BPA Parachuting Regula-tions, which safeguard us in the sport were largely his doing.

My thanks are also due to Pauline Barrett and Jerry Birkin, who translated my semi-illiterate scrawl into typescript, to George Russell for his excellent line illustrations, to John Meacock for his valuable advice and finally, to the numerous BPA members who have assisted me with ideas for this, the revised edition of what was originally published in 1971.

Charles Shea-Simonds
Leeds

Chapter 1

Your First Descent

You wake up with a start. The sun is streaming through the window and there is a strange quiet which contrasts vividly with the solid drumming of the rain on the roof the previous evening. Thoughts tumble with abandon through your brain: 'Am I really going to parachute today?' 'Will I remember all I've been taught?' 'What will I feel like just before I go?' and of course, 'Why in heaven's name did I start this ludicrous sport anyway?'

Soon, however, after a hasty mug of tea and having donned a pair of white overalls and a stout pair of rubber-soled boots, you're adjusting your main parachute harness assisted by one of the more experienced members of the club. Your instructor walks over to you. 'You're number two in the second stick – everything OK?' You grin, hoping it looks brave but suspecting it doesn't. 'Yes, fine,' you reply unconvincingly.

'First stick line up over here' the instructor shouts and seven jumpers gather together and wait to be checked out. At this moment the roar of two Gypsy Aero engines increases as a De Havilland Rapide taxies from behind the hangar. The first stick has now been checked and they are walking towards the aircraft while the instructor gives final directions to the two club members who are to lay out the fluorescent target cross.

The students clamber up on to the port wing and struggle unfamiliarly through the small door into the aircraft. Moments later the elegant bi-plane taxies out and lines up for take-off. The engine roar increases and after gathering speed down the runway the elderly aeroplane lifts gently from the tarmac.

You are aware of the tension building up inside you and you give a start as someone says 'Next stick over here.' Above you the Rapide drones higher and heads around you look skyward. Overhead a

11

brightly coloured strip of paper, thrown by the instructor, flutters earthwards and you suddenly remember being told about the 'streamer' to calculate the speed and direction of the wind.

'Helmets on!' and you find you're all fingers and thumbs trying to fasten the strap. 'Here, let me help,' says a cheery voice and you're relieved to let him take over.

'There he goes!' and looking up you see the Rapide is already running over a second time and a figure drops away with an orange and white canopy blossoming open above it. Then another . . . and a third. The aircraft breaks away with a sudden surge of engine noise.

'Is that tight enough?' and you realise the voice is speaking to you. You look down at your chest strap. 'Oh – yes thanks,' your reply doesn't sound in the least like you.

The aircraft starts its second jump-run and seconds later two more figures are rocking gently under inflated canopies. Again the Rapide drones over and the final two parachutes billow open. All too soon the aircraft is gliding in over the boundary hedge, gracefully touches down and then taxies towards where you're standing.

There's no backing down now and already the instructor is checking the stick. Helmet, capewell releases, chest straps, reserve parachute hooks, ripcord pins, tie down and leg straps are all checked from the front, followed by static line stowage, break ties and elastics from the back.

Adorned with 45 lbs of parachute, your walk to the aircraft seems ungainly – in fact it is, and you are suddenly aware of your instructor's final briefing before you clamber aboard.

'Take your time in the aircraft and protect your reserve handle as you move – I'll do the rest. Make sure your static line runs clear and remember, left foot, left hand, right foot, right hand as you get on to the wing. Look at me when you're set to go. When I give the word, throw your head back and assume a good arch and stable position. If you see me as you fall away I guarantee you're in a good position. And remember I want you to shout the count so loud that the pilot can hear it. The decision to throw the reserve is yours but don't hang about if you have to use it. Finally when you land be sure you're turned into wind – that's facing the buildings on the far side of the airfield.'

You clamber aboard wondering if you'll remember it all and now you're sitting on the floor facing your instructor who is in the seat by the door. 'Bill . . . three runs at two five, three on the first pass, two on the second and two on the third. Same run as before,' yells the instructor. A thumbs up from the pilot indicates he's understood and with a rise in engine note, the brakes are released and the Rapide lurches forward. At the downwind end of the runway each engine is run up in turn to check for a possible mag. drop and moments later you're careering down the tarmac, the tail lifts off and suddenly you're airborne. The aircraft banks to the left and you glimpse a kaleidoscopic blur of runway and green grass through the open door.

On the bulkhead behind your instructor's seat you catch sight of an altimeter whose hands turn slowly clockwise, relentlessly recording the climb to dropping height. At 1,000 feet the instructor stands up, takes the static line hook from the parachutist on your right and snaps it on to the wire cable secured on the roof of the cabin. He then takes yours and repeats the operation, allowing you to tug at it to check it's holding fast. This seems strangely reassuring as already you're trying to imagine what it will be like when the time comes.

Fields and trees slide past beneath but the pleasure of the flight is lost on you. You swallow hard, thinking to yourself, 'It must be all right, thousands of people have done it before.' Then . . . 'But this time it's me – that's the difference!'

The instructor is now leaning out of the door, his face contorted into ripples by the slipstream, making sure the aircraft is on the correct run in. He's obviously satisfied as he pulls himself in tapping his knees as he does so. This is the sign for you to kneel facing the door. You struggle to your knees assisted by those behind you, while your instructor clears the static and leans over you to check once again the break ties on the back of your parachute pack.

The instructor's again leaning out of the door; you must be near now as he's looking straight down. He pulls himself in and yells, 'Five right!', the aircraft yaws to the right and your stomach tries to go with it. He checks again but this time . . . 'CUT' and the noise of the engines suddenly dies. The instructor points towards the door and your neighbour clambers up and out. He's on the wing gripping the strut now and looking helplessly towards the instructor. The slipstream tears at his overalls as the instructor taps him on the knee with a simultaneous 'GO . . .' He drops away in a floundering of arms and legs.

Suddenly it's your moment of truth, your heart feels as if it's trying to break out, it's pounding so hard. You grope for the door guided by strong hands. The slipstream hits you and you grab the strut firmly.

All you are aware of is a voice saying 'This is it!' – then 'GO!' and automatically you fling out your arms and legs as you've practised so many times on the ground. You're falling . . . falling . . . fall . . . then a firm tug at your shoulders and your legs swing down below you. You look up and see orange and white blossoming above and the aircraft banking away. 'I've done it . . . I've done it . . . hell, I forgot to count . . .' Exhilaration takes over and momentarily you forget what's expected of you next. Suddenly it's quiet and you're on your own, swinging gently under that beautiful canopy. You look about you . . . there's the airfield behind you . . . look up and grasp the steering toggles. You pull down on the left-hand toggle and swing round in that direction until you face the field. There's the target cross and you see two ant-like figures standing nearby. You turn the canopy round again just to experience being master of your parachute.

'No. 2 . . . pull down on your right toggle.' An amplified voice reaches you. No. 2 . . . that's you . . . which one did he say? 'Pull down on your *right* toggle . . . that's it . . . keep it there.' The buildings appear to be getting a good deal larger and you look immediately below you to see the inviting green of the grass. 'Keep your feet and knees tight together No. 2 . . . that's it' as you concentrate on your 'parachuting position'. You appear to be close to landing now. Suddenly the ground rushes up at you and . . . Bang! you arrive firmly in an untidy heap. You look up in time to see the orange and white nylon cascade about you. You lie there unbelievably unhurt and finding it difficult to hoist in the fact that you've actually made your first parachute descent.

*   *   *   *

Well, your first parachute descent might be something like that but even if it isn't one thing is certain: it will be unforgettable.
In the following chapters you will be guided through your ground training, your first descent and beyond.
However, before you can even start your ground training programme there is the irksome formality of documentation to be undertaken. The next chapter will tell you what is required.

Chapter 2

Documentation

Before you make your first descent certain documentation must be completed for a variety of reasons. This chapter explains the documentation required and the reasons for it.

Initially two documents are required and these are:

(a) Membership of the British Parachute Association.

(b) A Doctor's Certificate.

First, membership of the British Parachute Association: the BPA controls Sport Parachuting in Great Britain and is thus responsible to the Civil Aviation Authority for all aspects of the sport. The BPA employs a full time Secretary General and Secretariat at its offices at Kimberley House, 47 Vaughan Way, Leicester LE1 4SG, and its policies are directed by an elected Council. The BPA has a Safety and Training Sub-Committee which is made up of the country's most experienced parachutists. Its function is to advise on all matters of training and safety and to revise and amend the BPA Parachuting Regulations as necessary. The BPA appoints qualified instructors and ensures that they control sport parachuting in accordance with its Parachuting Regulations. The BPA is also responsible for the organisation of the National Parachute Championships, the selection of the National Team and its training for the World Championships and other international events. The Association publishes its own bi-monthly magazine, *Sport Parachutist*, which provides articles and photographs on all aspects of the sport, and a means of communicating up-to-date information to its members. It is required by law that all sport parachutists are covered by insurance for third party liability, and to this end the BPA covers its members for third party liability to the sum of £100,000. This policy is held in the BPA offices, and the service is a most useful one; providing you are parachuting in accordance with BPA Parachuting Regulations, the BPA will be financially responsible for damage to property or persons that you might cause as a direct result of a parachute descent. The Association also maintains an up-to-date register of active parachute clubs throughout the country and thus you can be put in touch with the club nearest to where you live by contacting the Secretary General at the address given above.

So, for an annual subscription of £4.21 (which includes an entry fee of 54p) you are benefited in the following three basic ways:

(a) You are given world-wide third party insurance cover up to £100,000.

(b) You receive the magazine *Sport Parachutist* six times a year, and, most important of all

(c) You receive the services of an Association which is constantly striving to better the sport and ensure your safety in parachuting.

Your club should be able to provide you with a BPA Membership application form but if not, you can obtain one direct from the Secretary General. Once you receive the form, you should fill it in carefully, making sure the indemnities on the reverse side are signed as applicable. Your BPA membership is valid for twelve months from 1st April annually. You will receive a reminder when your subscription is due and remember, you should not parachute unless your membership is valid. The second form essential before your first descent is a doctor's certificate. Blank certificates may be obtained from the BPA office, but you may use a typed or duplicated one if you wish. You should see your local doctor for your medical, and sometimes payment is necessary, but in the majority of cases it is not required as the medical is such a simple one. On the BPA certificate there are some notes for the examining doctor, and these are reproduced here:

'Parachutists make descents from unpressurised aircraft at heights of between two thousand and twelve thousand feet above sea level without using oxygen. They must open their parachutes at a safe height above the ground and be prepared to take emergency action if their main parachute fails to open correctly. They should, therefore, be of an emotionally stable type.

During landing there are forces to be absorbed by the body approximately equivalent to jumping from a platform four and one half feet from the ground. Depending on the weight of the parachutist, weather conditions and other factors, the landing force may be greater than this equivalent.

The examinee must be in good general health and possess a sound musculo-skeletal system. The lower limbs usually accept the brunt of the landing force.

The minimum visual acuity of both eyes with or without glasses which is acceptable is 6/12 and the candidate must not be red/green colour blind. Hearing must be normal and it should be remembered that chronic sinusitis or otitis media is not compatible with rapid changes of air pressure that will occur during the descent.

The presence of any of the following conditions make a person unfit to parachute: diabetes and other 'glandular dysfunction', epilepsy, 'fainting attacks' or a history of psychiatric disorder. Any history of skull fracture, concussion or brain damage should be assessed most carefully, for in the course of landing the head may strike the ground with force, and brain damage tends to be cumulative. In cases of doubt a normal E EG pattern must be present.'

The format for the doctor's certificate is reproduced here:

Has the candidate any condition which in your opinion *might* interfere with his/her capacity to parachute safely?....................

Are you the candidate's usual practitioner?..............................

I am of the opinion that Mr/Mrs/Miss.....................is medically fit to make parachute descents.

Signed.......................   Address ....

Date ....

The doctor's certificate is valid for two years from the date of issue. After two years, or after any serious illness or injury, you should have another medical and a new certificate.

I shall now deal with documents not essential to your first descent, but which you will require as you progress with the sport.

The first of these (and you will be given this by your instructor or club) is your BPA Category Card. It shows each of the ten categories of sport parachutist (as outlined in Chapter 11) and it will be dated and signed by your instructor when you reach the standard of each category. Once you have made your first two or three descents and have decided that you are going to continue with the sport, you are obliged to record all your parachute descents in a log book. Log books may be obtained from the BPA office. price approximately £1.00. They contain spaces for 200 descents and record the following details of each descent: Number, Date and Time; Dropping Zone; Aircraft Type; Qualified

Parachutist or Pilot signature and Certificate/Licence Number; Back Chute Type; Altitude; Delay in Seconds; Manoeuvres; Distance from Target; Wind in m.p.h., and Remarks.

Every descent should be recorded in detail as soon as possible after it is made. Until you have qualified for a 'C' Certificate it is important that your instructor should sign each entry and record relevant observations in the 'Remarks' column. A 'C' Certificate is granted when a parachutist no longer needs instructor supervision, and is issued by the BPA.

You should ensure that your log book is an accurate history of your parachuting progression. This will enable any new instructor to assess at a glance from dates, heights and comments what type of descent you should be making.

Finally, try to fill in your log book as neatly and carefully as you can, for later you will find it very satisfying to recall previous descents and nothing is worse than leaving them scruffily recorded.

The next two documents are issued on behalf of the Royal Aero Club of the United Kingdom (agents for the Federation Aeronautique International) by the BPA.

The first is the FAI Parachutist Certificate. This is an internationally recognised certificate of agreed parachuting standards. Thus, if you wish to parachute abroad this certificate is a most useful document to be able to produce.

The standards required are as follows:

Certificate A (1) Have made at least 10 jumps.

Certificate B (1) Have made at least 25 free fall jumps including 15 stable delays of at least 10 seconds, 5 stable delays of at least 20 seconds, one stable delay of at least 30 seconds.

(2) Demonstrate ability to hold heading during free fall, i.e. prevent spin.

(3) Have landed within 50 yards of centre of a target on 5 jumps with delays of 20 seconds or longer.

Certificate C (1) Have made at least 50 free fall jumps.

(2) Have qualified as BPA Category VIII.

(3) Complete two alternate 360° flat turns to left and right in free fall in 7 seconds or less.

(4) Have landed within 30 yards of centre of a target on 15 jumps with delays of 20 seconds or longer.

Certificate D (1) Have made at least 200 free fall jumps including 100 stable delays of at least 20 seconds, 50 stable delays of at least 30 seconds, 20 stable delays of at least 45 seconds, 10 stable delays of at least 50 seconds.

(2) Complete two alternate 360° flat turns to left and right in free fall in 6 seconds or less.

(3) Demonstrate control in free fall on vertical, horizontal and longitudinal axes of body.

(4) Have landed within 20 yards of centre of a target on 20 jumps with delays of at least 30 seconds.

Once again, you will be able to obtain the relevant application form from the BPA should your club not be able to produce one. The form must be countersigned by a BPA instructor to certify that you have reached the standard required for the certificate for which you are applying. You must send with your application to the BPA two photographs ($1\frac{1}{2}'' \times 2''$) of yourself, together with a fee of £1 + VAT; this sum covers the issue of the certificate and initial endorsements, any further endorsements costing thirty pence each.

The BPA are also responsible for issuing FAI Parachute Competitors Licences which you require if you wish to compete in parachuting championships both at home and abroad. The application form is obtained as for the Parachutist's Certificate and should be sent completed in the same way to the BPA, a BPA instructor's signature certifying your competence to compete and an initial fee of fifty pence + VAT. The licence is valid for twelve months from 1st January and can be renewed for a further thirty pence + VAT.

The remaining documents can be dealt with very quickly. Once you own your own parachute you must keep a log-card (for which there is no set format) to record when you pack the 'chute and any modifications or repairs that you carry out. Following from this is a Packing Certificate which will be granted to you when your instructor considers that you are competent to pack parachutes without supervision. The final certificate that you might receive is that signed by the Secretary General certifying that you are a qualified BPA Instructor, having been successfully examined by two BPA Advanced Instructors who are Instructor Examiners.

Finally, mention must be made of The Air Navigation Order which, in Article 38 prohibits the making of parachute descents over the United Kingdom. To exempt sport parachutists from this article each Club obtains annually from the Civil Aviation Authority 'a Parachuting Exemption. Initially this need not concern you, but it may be that, with your gaining of experience, you are asked to assist in club administration, and that the obtaining of the club's exemption may become your responsibility. Application should be made to one of the three regional offices of the CAA Field Organisation depending upon where your club is situated geographically:

(a)   Civil Aviation Authority
      Operations
      Broomhouse Drive
      Edinburgh EH11 3XE
This address covers the whole of Scotland.

(b)   Civil Aviation Authority
      Operations
      Mersey House
      The Strand
      Liverpool L2 7PZ
This address covers Northern Ireland, Wales and the North of
      England above an imaginary line drawn from the Bristol
      Channel to the Wash.

(c)   Civil Aviation Authority
      Operations
      Heston Aerodrome
      Hounslow
      Middlesex
This address covers the remainder of the country.

It will probably be some time before you are involved with corresponding with the CAA so let us, in the meantime, examine the parachute equipment that you will be using.

Chapter 3

Equipment

Before dealing with parachute equipment itself and how it operates, it is logical to cover the items of personal clothing required for the sport. A one-piece overall or flying suit is desirable, firstly to prevent any pieces of material flapping loosely as a result of wearing two or more articles of clothing, and secondly to save undue wear on your normal clothing which might come about through constant practice of parachute landings and moving around in the somewhat cramped and sometimes dirty interiors of light aircraft. Of course, one can buy a proper jumpsuit designed for the job but, as with much of the equipment to be mentioned, there is little point in spending unnecessarily large sums of money until you are certain you are going to carry on with the sport.

Until you qualify for a 'C' Certificate it is advisable that you wear white (either overalls or jumpsuit); the reason for this is that it enables your instructor to observe distinctly your parachuting performance. Once you have gained a 'C' Certificate you may wear a jumpsuit of any colour, but bright colours are advised to avoid the possibility of mid-air collisions.

The next item is a helmet. Any peakless motor cycle helmet approved by the British Standards Institute or equivalent foreign organisation is suitable. A word of warning here, however, seems relevant. You will be wearing a helmet to protect your head, firstly when leaving the aircraft, secondly in free fall (in the unlikely event of someone careering into you), and thirdly during the landing itself. No helmet will last indefinitely and a parachutist's helmet will tend to take more of a bashing than one worn by a motor cyclist, who would probably replace it anyway if it took a severe knock. I therefore believe that once you have taken up the sport a really good helmet is a sensible buy; but of course it's your head!

As all your parachute landings will be taken on your feet (preferably!), the type of boot you wear is important. Your boots should be strong, well-fitting, ankle boots with rubber soles to avoid slipping and ideally the soles should be smooth. They should *not* have hooks for the laces as these might foul rigging lines in the event of a poor body position during canopy deployment; therefore climbing or skiing boots are not suitable. Here again excellent boots designed especially for the sport can be obtained. They are expensive but if you wear them just while you parachute they will last for a good many years.

Goggles should normally be worn (remember bits of grit or a fly in your eye can be very uncomfortable) and many types are suitable. They should provide the best possible vision and if you wear glasses you can purchase goggles which can be worn over them. A little individual experiment here will probably be required, for example, to decide whether to wear them with the strap inside or outside the helmet.

Suitable gloves are an aid to parachuting under all conditions and should be always worn in cold weather. They should be of soft leather to allow plenty of movement. Really heavy gauntlets are not suitable.

Now for the parachutes themselves. Yes, you're required to be equipped with two parachutes attached to a common harness. First is the 'main' parachute which you will wear on your back. Initially you will use a flat circular type of canopy which will not be less than 28 feet in diameter. There are other types of canopy designed specifically for sport parachuting but in this chapter only the flat circular type will be discussed as the basic terms and operation for all varieties are much the same.

To enable you to understand the operative parts of the parachute you should study Figure 1. From the top, the 'pilot 'chute' (sometimes called the 'extractor' or 'drogue') is the small parachute that pulls the rest of the parachute from the pack. It has a strong spring built into it which ejects the pilot'chute clear of your back when the pack is opened. Many parachutists prefer to use two instead of one. This gives a more positive opening than just one with a weak spring but if this system is used the two pilot 'chutes should be connected to a common bridle line. The 'bridle line' is a strong nylon cord (normally of about 1,000 lbs breaking strain) that connects the pilot 'chute to the sleeve, and the sleeve is attached to the apex of the parachute by the 'sleeve retaining line'. The 'apex' of the parachute is the hole at the top where the rigging lines can also be seen. The 'deployment sleeve' is a long sock-like device which

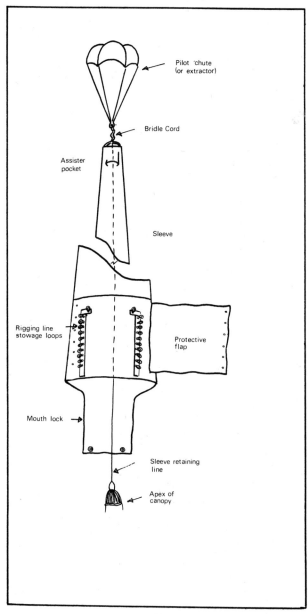

Fig. 1. The parts of the parachute

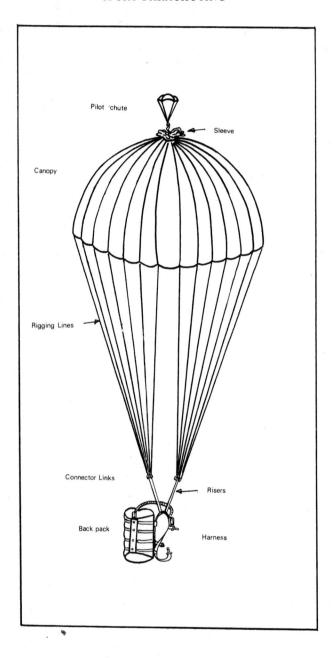

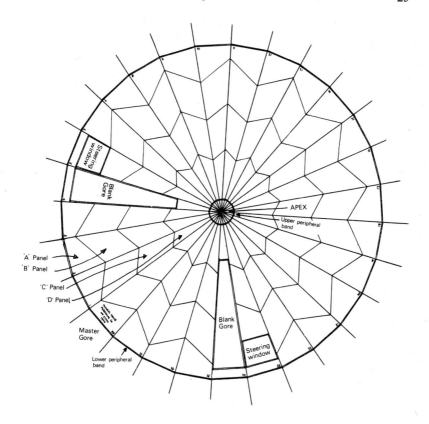

Fig. 2. The 28ft flat circular canopy modified to a double 'L'

Note: Lines 1-7 go to the left rear riser
lines 8-14 go to the left front riser
lines 15-21 go to the right front riser
lines 22-28 go to the right rear riser

The two steering lines are attached to lines 6 and 23 respectively contains the parachute canopy to ensure that the rigging lines have been deployed before the canopy starts to inflate and that the opening is relatively gradual, thus reducing the shock to your person and also prolonging the life of the canopy. The sleeve is normally made of a strong linen fabric so that when it slides off the canopy during deployment the nylon is not burnt through friction. At the bottom of the sleeve is a flap of material with a hole in each lower corner; this is known as the 'mouth lock', and its function is to prevent airflow entering the sleeve until the rigging lines have been pulled out of the retaining bands. The 'retaining bands' are elastic bands that are attached to nylon loops sewn on to the lower end of the sleeve, in which the rigging lines are stowed.

The parachute canopy is made of nylon and the amount of air the material will allow to pass through it is called the 'porosity' of the canopy. A low-porosity canopy, affectionately called a 'Lo-Po' allows less air to pass through it than a high-porosity canopy. A normal 28-foot diameter flat circular canopy has 28 gores. The 'gore' is that wedge-shaped part of the canopy between each rigging line. In turn each gore is divided into four 'panels' from the bottom lettered A, B, C and D panels. You will notice from Figure 2 that the seams between each panel are at a different angle on adjacent gores; this gives added strength to the manufacture of the canopy. Each gore can be easily identified by a number (obviously from 1 to 28) which is to be found in the bottom right-hand corner. This number also identifies the rigging line. Around the apex of the canopy (at the top) is a heavy band of material known as the upper peripheral band, and the heavy band around the bottom of the canopy is known as the lower peripheral band. The 'rigging lines' (or 'suspension lines') are the lines which join the canopy to the harness. Although there appear to be 28 rigging lines, this is not actually so since there are in fact 14 whole rigging lines which run continuously from the harness, up through the canopy, over the apex, down through the canopy again on the opposite side and back to the harness. Each rigging line, again made of nylon, has a breaking strain of about 500 lbs, and 28×500 lbs adds up to a lot of breaking strain! The rigging lines start and finish at the 'connector links' which are four metal links that each connect seven rigging lines to a 'riser'. The risers are pieces of nylon webbing about 30 inches long, $1\frac{3}{4}$ inches wide and having about 6,500 lbs breaking strain. The four risers are, in fact, only two separate lengths of webbing which have a set of connector

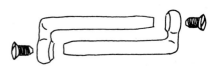

C. Set of Connector Links
    3,000 lbs Tensile Strength

B. Reserve 'D' Ring
    5,000 lbs Tensile Strength

stable) Snap Ejector
Tensile Strength

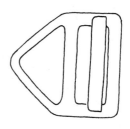

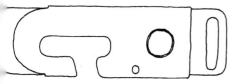

D. Adjustable Harness V Ring
    2,500 lbs Tensile Strength

E. Static Line Sliding Clip
    1,750 lbs Tensile Strength

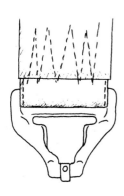

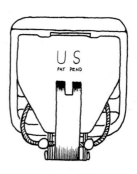

US
PAT PEND

F. Capewell Release (Male)
    5,000 lbs Tensile Strength

Fig. 3. Parachuting hardware

G. Capewell Release (Female)
    ('1½ - shot' type)

links at each end. In the middle, each riser is stitched around the male part of the Capewell release. The 'Capewell release' is the normal method of connecting the canopy to the harness and the female part of the Capewell is an integral part of the harness. There are three types of the female part of the Capewell and they have become known as the '2 shot', the '1½ shot' and the '1 shot'. To release the two shot Capewell, the cover is pulled down revealing two opposing buttons. The thumb and forefinger are then used to press these two buttons together and pull down the second flap which allows the male part of the Capewell to break away. The one and a half shot is simpler to use–when the cover is pulled down a wire loop springs out. When this loop is tugged firmly using your thumb only the second flap is pulled down allowing the male part of the Capewell to break away as before. The one shot is simpler still–the pulling of the cover downwards is all that is required to release the male part of the Capewell. Initially you will probably find the two shot Capewell on your harness. The merits of the 1½ shot and one shot will be discussed in a later chapter.

The harness is made of the same type of nylon webbing as the risers. The harness should be as tight a fit as possible without being uncomfortable. You will normally find 7 points of adjustment on the harness and these are the two back adjustments, the two body adjustments, the two leg straps and the chest strap. Figure 3 shows you the types of buckle and other hardware to be found on a parachute harness. Sewn around the harness just below one of the Capewell releases you will find the ripcord pocket. This is self-explanatory: it is an elastic-sided nylon pocket which houses the ripcord handle itself when the parachute is packed. From the top of the ripcord pocket, the ripcord housing runs to the top flap of the pack. This housing is a flexible metal cover through which the ripcord itself runs. The ripcord is a cable of braided stainless steel with a handle on one end and a series of pins on the other which actually lock the pack closed.

The pack is that part of the parachute which houses the canopy, sleeve and rigging lines together on your back. It will normally have a small top and bottom flap (each with a ripcord cone attached) and two large side flaps. The flap on one side will have a grommet at the top, then two cones and another grommet at the bottom. The other flap has a stiffened wide edge with a line of four grommets running down it.

Each pack normally has four 'elastics' or 'pack opening bands' (sometimes called 'bungees'). Each of the pack opening bands runs across the

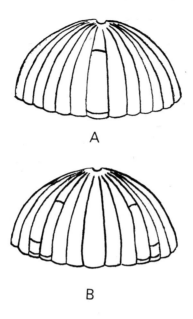

A

B

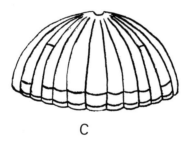

C

Fig. 4. Parachute modifications.
(a) single blank (rarely used)
(b) double 'L'
(c) 7 gore 'TU'
(b and c very common)

back of the pack and a hook on each end is hooked into an eye sewn to each side flap when the rig is ready to jump.

You will probably find the equipment you use initially will be government surplus equipment (usually American). Basically this is because it is cheaper than equipment manufactured specifically for the sport. However, before surplus equipment can be used for sport parachuting certain modifications have to be made. The sleeve is, in fact, a modification in itself for the surplus parachute would not originally have had one. All modifications must be carried out by a qualified 'rigger', (rigger being the name given to a person who maintains parachute equipment) or by a parachute manufacturer.

The most important modification is the removal of fabric from parts of the canopy to enable it to be steered. Details of how this works are given in Chapter 8. The important points to remember here are that no more than the equivalent of three gores should be removed and under no circumstances must the peripheral bands be modified. You will find that you will probably start with a Double L modification and then progress to a TU. These two are the most common, although you may well come across others; and they are illustrated in Figure 4.

The next modification is the fitting of the reserve parachute 'D' rings to the harness. It is not uncommon to find 'D' rings which have been fitted incorrectly and if you purchase your own equipment this is a point about which you must consult an instructor. Basically, however, there should be no likelihood of the 'D' rings being ripped or torn away in the event of the reserve parachute having to be deployed at terminal velocity. (Having mentioned terminal velocity it seems logical to define it at this stage: terminal velocity is the ultimate speed at which the human body travels in free fall, normally reached after about ten seconds, and is usually about 120 miles per hour or 176 ft/sec. This figure varies depending on the weight and surface area of individual parachutists.)

Finally, two more 'D' rings are sewn on the bottom of the pack (one on each side). These are for the reserve tie-down which will be discussed shortly.

Now it is important for you to know how the parachute works and to understand it fully, you should study Figure 5.

When the parachute has been packed (this procedure is described fully in Chapter 10), the pack is kept closed by the ripcord pins which pass one through each cone, each cone protruding through a grommet.

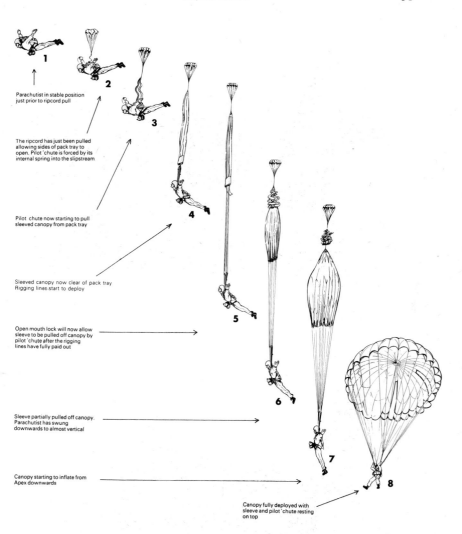

Parachutist in stable position just prior to ripcord pull

The ripcord has just been pulled allowing sides of pack tray to open. Pilot 'chute is forced by its internal spring into the slipstream

Pilot chute now starting to pull sleeved canopy from pack tray

Sleeved canopy now clear of pack tray Rigging lines start to deploy

Open mouth lock will now allow sleeve to be pulled off canopy by pilot 'chute after the rigging lines have fully paid out

Sleeve partially pulled off canopy. Parachutist has swung downwards to almost vertical

Canopy starting to inflate from Apex downwards

Canopy fully deployed with sleeve and pilot 'chute resting on top

CANOPY DEPLOYMENT

Fig. 5. Canopy deployment

Thus when the ripcord handle is pulled, the pins are withdrawn from the cones which allows the sides of the pack to open. In fact the sides are pulled forcibly open by the 4 pack opening bands on each side

The instant the pack opens the extractor 'chute is ejected from it by means of the spring inside

The flow of air past the body thus deploys the extractor 'chute

which in turn pulls the sleeve away from the pack.

When the sleeve is clear of the pack the rigging lines start to deploy from the elastic bands at its base

When the rigging lines free themselves from the top two elastic bands the sleeve mouth lock is opened by their final straightening

Now the sleeve is free to slide off and this allows the canopy to deploy.

The extractor 'chute is still pulling the sleeve and additional lift is given by the two pockets sewn on either side of it. The air flow now enters the bottom of the canopy and this airflow forces the sleeve from the last few feet. The canopy now deploys from the top downwards until the airflow has opened it completely. This whole sequence will take about 2 to 3 seconds.

The reserve parachute is in essence very much simpler. Initially you are likely to use a flat circular 24-foot canopy, which again will probably be government surplus. However, reserve canopies specially designed for the sport are becoming more popular; they vary slightly in design and are normally 26 feet in diameter. The modern reserve canopies have the two advantages of a low rate of descent combined with manoeuvrability. The standard 24-foot canopy has little control and is designed purely as a life-saver.

The parts of the reserve parachute are much the same as the main. Until you start using sophisticated main canopies your reserve parachute should not have an extractor 'chute and I shall go into the reasons for this in Chapter 7. The 24-foot reserve canopy has 24 gores and thus 24 rigging lines (or 12 complete lines running from connector link to opposite connector link). Some reserve parachutes have short risers (about 12″ long) which terminate in two hooks and on others the rigging lines go directly to the two hooks. These two hooks are used to attach the reserve to the 'D' rings on the main harness and should always be joined together by a length (about 10 inches) of 6,500 lb nylon webbing or the equivalent length and strength in 500 lb cord looped continuously between them. The reason for the hooks being joined is that in the unlikely event of one hook coming undone, the reserve canopy will remain inflated and attached to the main harness by the other hook on its own.

The reserve parachute has no sleeve to ensure that the opening, when required, is as fast as possible. The reserve pack has much in common with the main pack. There are four flaps which close around the packed canopy. As with the main, the pack is held together with the ripcord pins (normally two) inserted through two cones which in turn protrude through the grommets. With the absence of a sleeve the rigging lines are stowed in elastic bands attached to web loops in the pack tray itself. The reserve is operated by pulling the ripcord handle (normally located in a pocket on the top of the pack); this releases the cones from the grommets and the pack opening bands pull the flaps open, thus allowing the canopy to deploy. The sequence here is opposite to the main canopy deployment as the canopy pays out before the rigging lines. The reserve canopy thus opens considerably quicker than the main. The last part of the reserve parachute is the tie down. This is a web strap with a snap hook on each end and a buckle to adjust its length. Each snap hook (sometimes snap-ejectors) is hooked to the tie down 'D' rings at the base of the main pack. When pulled up tightly the tie down keeps the reserve flush against the body.

I have described the basic parachute equipment and of course it would be impossible to cover all the variations in equipment that you will meet. For instance, some sport parachutes have only three ripcord pins on the main pack; some foreign parachutes (e.g. French) do not have Capewell releases (the risers being an integral part of the harness) and some reserve parachutes have the ripcord handle located in a pocket on the top of the pack. But the basic principles remain the same. One significant variation is worth a particular mention, however, and this is the 'piggyback' rig. Originally designed in America, the 'piggyback' rig has the reserve mounted above the main on your back. There are a number of advantages to this system which will be covered in later chapters but the basic principle remains unchanged. The reserve is still attached to the same harness as the main and is operated by a ripcord handle stowed on the front of the main harness on the opposite side to the main ripcord handle. There is also a static line system in some 'piggyback' rigs which operates the reserve automatically if the main parachute is jettisoned, but more of this in Chapter 7.

Your first few descents will be made using a static line operated main parachute, the static line being a means of opening your parachute automatically. The system consists of the static line itself which is a line of 3,000 lb nylon webbing, 12-15 feet long, with a loop at one end and a sliding snap hook at the other. The principle is simple–instead of having the ripcord pins through the cones, a piece of 50 lb nylon thread is passed through each cone and tied firmly around the static line. The hook end is attached to a cable or strongpoint in the aircraft. When you fall away from the aircraft the static line pulls out and the weight of your body breaks the nylon ties and the canopy deploys as previously described. This deployment is assisted by having the loop on the end of the static line going inside the packed rig (between the third and fourth grommets) and attached to the loop on the base of the extractor 'chute with a further tie of 50 lb nylon cord or with Velcro tape. The static line therefore actually assists the pilot 'chute to pull the sleeve and canopy away from the pack. Here again you may find yourself using a main parachute assembly designed especially for static line jumping. This system does away with cones on the pack but has strong elastic loops instead. The loops are passed one through each grommet and ripcord pins from the end of the static line pass one through each elastic loop. Velcro tape is used instead of the final break-tie between the extractor 'chute and the static line. The disadvantage of this assembly is that it cannot be used for free fall but it is safe and easy to pack. I will be discussing the static line system further in later chapters.

Once you progress to free fall you will find yourself using instruments. The two instruments used are the altimeter and the stop-watch, the latter being of any robust, conventional type. The altimeter, however, should be of the non-sensitive type with a single sweep hand. Any conventional aircraft altimeter of the sensitive type with more than one hand should not be used. There are also altimeters specially designed for the sport, but whatever type it may be there are two points that should be remembered. Firstly, the altimeter is a delicate instrument that operates through change in barometric pressure with increase in altitude; it should, therefore, be treated with care. Secondly, all altimeters have a slight lag (about 50–100 feet) when the parachutist has reached terminal velocity. Many parachutists obtain surplus altimeters from various devious sources; if you do this, make sure you have your altimeter tested properly before you use it yourself. Any pilot will take it up for you and check it against the altimeter in his aircraft, if you ask him nicely! Instruments should be mounted where they can be clearly seen, either on a plate on the reserve parachute (if the latter is chest-mounted) or attached to the harness or mounted on the wrist; any of these methods is acceptable and is purely a matter of personal preference.

Finally, a word on automatic opening devices is necessary. Automatic opening devices vary considerably in design from those which operate the main parachute to those which operate the reserve, and from those that are fired ballistically to those that are fired with a spring. Like the altimeter, they function initially through change in barometric pressure (except those few available with short timing devices) and therefore require careful treatment. An automatic opening device should be used only as an emergency device and should not be relied upon for initial deployment of the main parachute. All A.O.Ds are very expensive and many people are still sceptical of them; however, many serious accidents have been prevented by their use and this cannot be overlooked. (See Chapter 7).

Simple maintenance and care of parachutes will be dealt with in Chapter 10 but all parachute equipment should be treated with care and respect. It almost goes without saying that the better you look after it, the better it will look after you.

Chapter 4

The Initial Training Programme

Having completed the various documentation described in Chapter 1 you are now ready to start your ground training. I cannot stress enough just how important your initial training is and, although much will depend on your instructor, a very great deal depends on you as you cannot afford to be anything less than thoroughly and completely trained in every respect. To enable you to attain this target you should approach your training with the following in mind.

Firstly, you must be completely dedicated. This sounds obvious but it is very frustrating for the instructor if one or two of his students are late for the morning's training session, or if one of them decides to skip the afternoon's training session because his girl friend wants to go to the cinema. In your initial training you cannot afford to miss anything.

Secondly, you should be physically fit. The majority of people could pass the medical but I do not believe that this is enough. To be mentally alert it helps considerably to be physically fit and you must be alert and fit to parachute. This does not mean that you have to be a superman (or supergirl!) but a little common sense is required; for instance, a gentle jog around the airfield never hurt anyone but it can help a great deal. Always get a good night's sleep and keep off the alcohol. When you are actually parachuting it is forbidden to consume alcohol until you have carried out your last jump of the day. It is also important that you avoid a drinking session during the evening before parachuting the following day. Alcohol dims your mental processes and slows your reactions so it is equally important to lay off during your ground training. Once you actually start parachuting you should not jump unless you feel fit in every way; even the common cold has its dangers due to the changes in atmospheric pressure to which you will be subjected.

Finally, you must have an inquiring mind. If anything your instructor tells you is not absolutely crystal clear in your own mind then ask him to run through it again. He may well tell you to do something but he may not give you the reason for it—make sure you ask him. Watch other parachutists and learn from their mistakes. Never be afraid to grill the really experienced parachutist for additional knowledge; read everything you can on the subject and study all available photographs. Much of the practical side of your ground training you can practise away from your club; don't restrict your training to the airfield alone. In fact, however much it may peeve your relatives and friends, you should eat, sleep, think and talk parachuting during your initial training! Your initial ground training will be carried out in accordance with the BPA Minimum Ground Training Programme, which is as follows:

1. *Orientation*   *30 minutes*
   (*a*) Documentation (check BPA Membership, Insurance, Medical Certificate, BPA Classification Card etc.).
   (*b*) Outline of Training Syllabus.
   (*c*) Routine Safety Instructions to be observed with aircraft (crossing runways etc.).
   (*d*) Orientation flight (if desired).
2. *Introduction*   *30 minutes*
   (*a*) Safety Regulations.
   (*b*) Equipment and dress.
   (*c*) Introduction to aircraft to be used in training.
   (*d*) Wind drift determination.
   (*e*) Exit technique (stability).
   (*f*) Emergency procedures.
   (*g*) Canopy handling.
   (*h*) Landing techniques.
   (*j*) Parachute packing.
3. *Familiarisation with Parachutes*   *90 minutes*
   (*a*) The anatomy of the main assembly.
   (*b*) The anatomy of the reserve assembly.
   (*c*) The functioning of main and reserve parachutes.
   (*d*) Parachute fitting.
   (*e*) Pre-planning a parachute descent.
   (*f*) Equipment checking procedure.
4. *Familiarisation with Aircraft*   *30 minutes*
   (*a*) Safety checks.

(b) Procedures for entering and exiting with particular reference to guarding reserve parachutes.

(c) Static line procedure.

(d) Signals and words of command in the air.

5. *Aircraft Exits*   *60 minutes*
   (a) Preparatory commands and signals and actions.
   (b) Move into exit position.
   (c) Position after exit (stable position).
   (d) Counting, count follow-through and, later, dummy ripcord pulls (DRCP).

6. *Emergency Procedures*   *90 minutes*
   (a) Verbal count – static line.
   (b) Verbal count – free fall.
      (1) Count prior to ripcord pull.
      (2) Count after ripcord pull.
   (c) Check of main canopy immediately after opening.
   (d) Recognition of malfunctions.
   (e) Corrective actions.
      (1) Total malfunction.
      (2) Partial malfunctions (stable and spinning).
   (f) Drill period using suspended harness.

7. *Canopy Handling*   *60 minutes*
   (using suspended harness if possible)
   (a) Check canopy.
   (b) Orientation with ground:
      (1) Grasp toggles.
      (2) Ascertain location over ground, target and drift.
      (3) Work to wind line (zigzag method, etc. to obtain).
      (4) Check vertical angle of descent (hold or run).
      (5) Avoidance of obstacles (do not become intent on target).
      (6) Suspended harness drill period.
   (c) Prepare to land:
      (1) Altitude to adopt landing position: approx 150 ft (8–10 seconds).
      (2) Body position, face into wind.
      (3) Obeying ground instructions if loudspeaker equipment is available.

8. *Parachute Landing Falls*   *90 minutes*
   (*a*) Types:
       (1) Normal (front, back, side).
       (2) Tree.
       (3) Power Line.
       (4) Water.
   (*b*) Five (5) points of body contact.
   (*c*) Recovery from drag:
       (1) Hit, Roll, Recover, Run.
       (2) Pulling lines.
       (3) Capewell.
9. *Field Rolling the Parachute*   *30 minutes*
   (*a*) Chain lines.
   (*b*) Sleeve over canopy.
   (*c*) Close one side flap with pack-opening bands.
   (*d*) Secure all equipment and move to packing area.
10. *Dropping Zone Duties*   *30 minutes*
    (*a*) Responsibility.
    (*b*) Control.
    (*c*) Rotation of Personnel.
11. *Parachute Packing Instruction (Backpacks only)*   *3 hours*
12. *Testing—all phases*   *60 minutes*

Summary

Subject	Duration—hours
1. Orientation	$\frac{1}{2}$
2. Introduction	$\frac{1}{2}$
3. Familiarisation with Parachutes	$1\frac{1}{2}$
4. Familiarisation with Aircraft	$\frac{1}{2}$
5. Aircraft Exits	1
6. Emergency Procedures	$1\frac{1}{2}$
7. Canopy Handling	1
8. Parachute Landing Falls	$1\frac{1}{2}$
9. Field Rolling the Parachute	$\frac{1}{2}$
10. Dropping Zone Duties	$\frac{1}{2}$
11. Parachute Packing Instruction	3
12. Testing	1
Total:	13 hours

I shall now run through this programme and deal with the sections that are not covered in the chapters that follow. I must stress that this programme and the times given for each subject are the bare minimum necessary for an above-average student, and therefore your instructor may well spend longer on it to satisfy himself that you are fully trained. You will probably find that your parachute club operates in co-operation with a flying club and therefore it is important that you know how to behave on an airfield. Each flying club has its own set of rules and no doubt your instructor will brief you about the local rules at your club; however, the following apply on any airfield.

Never smoke in hangars or in close proximity of aircraft. The combination of aircraft dope and aviation fuel is a very real fire risk.

Be careful when handling light aircraft. They will be covered in either fabric or a thin alloy and damage is very easily done. Any pilot will gladly show where it's safe to push an aircraft or which parts you may use as a step to get in.

If an aircraft has its engine running, or is taxiing, always stand where the pilot can see you; remember, his visibility is probably more restricted than in the average car.

You should always know which is the duty runway and normally this will be the runway running roughly in the same direction as the wind. Remember, light aircraft always land and take off into the wind so if you have to cross the duty runway, the most important way to look is down wind. On some airfields you will not be allowed to cross the duty runway, but if you do, you should stop at least twenty yards short, kneel down (so any pilot landing can clearly see your intention) and check carefully that there are no aircraft in the circuit. When all is clear you should move briskly across. If a pilot has to over-shoot and make another circuit because of your dithering close to the duty runway, quite rightly he'll be a trifle irate!

The flying fraternity always regard parachutists as being slightly insane as they cannot understand anybody in their right mind wanting to leave a perfectly serviceable aircraft in flight. But whatever their views, always try to co-operate with them. Parachuting tends to be difficult without aircraft and the characters who fly them!

An orientation flight is a good idea if you've never flown before, (it's amazing the number of parachutists who hadn't before their first descent!) so be sure to tell your instructor if you haven't.

At an early stage of your ground training you will be introduced to Safety Regulations. I have set out Safety Regulations for you in Appendix A. They form Part Three of BPA Parachuting Regulations 1967 and must be observed completely by all BPA Affiliated Clubs and Centres. Occasionally there is a need for Safety Regulations to be amended as a result of new techniques and, when necessary, amendments will be produced by the Training and Safety Committee of the BPA

Initially, however, you should know that Sport Parachuting within BPA affiliated clubs and centres should be conducted under the following ten basic rules:

First   Under arrangements made by a BPA approved instructor who has been nominated as the Club Chief Instructor (CCI) and who is normally present when parachuting is in progress. (Obviously where a club has more than one instructor, the Club Chief Instructor, normally the most experienced, will assume overall responsibility for a student's training in that club).

Second   By parachutists who are in every respect fit, trained, dressed, equipped and briefed to undertake the descent planned.

Third   When an adequate ground control organisation is in operation (I go into more detail on DZ Control later in this chapter).

Fourth   With an approved pilot, and a jumpmaster qualified to dispatch the parachutist concerned. (Basically, an approved pilot is a pilot who has over 100 hours flying solo or in command of an aircraft and who has been tested by a parachute instructor on the techniques involved. These techniques will be covered in Chapter 5 and the qualifications of jumpmasters in Chapter 11).

Fifth   With parachutes in good condition, safe in all respects, correctly packed, well-fitted and inspected before emplaning.

Sixth   From an authorised aircraft suitably equipped and prepared for parachuting (this is covered in Chapter 5).

Seventh   When weather conditions are suitable. Limitations in weather conditions are basically as follows:

(*a*) *Wind*–Maximum surface wind speeds for the various categories of parachutists are given in Appendix A. As a student you will not parachute if the surface wind exceeds 10 m.p.h. (9 knots or 4·5 metres per second).

(b) *Cloud*–You will not parachute if the cloud base is less than 2,500 feet above ground level and you will not intentionally drop or be dropped through cloud. The whole of the ground between the drop zone and where you leave the aircraft must be visible.

(c) *Visibility*–You are only allowed to parachute in VMC (Visual Meteorological Conditions) i.e. a horizontal visibility of at least five nautical miles. (Parachuting at night is covered in Chapter 17.)

Eighth   On to an approved DZ (drop zone). (Normally an airfield or an open area of *at least* 600 yards in diameter free from major hazards (i.e. buildings, roads, wooded areas etc.) constitutes an unrestricted DZ suitable for student parachuting. (Restricted DZs will be dealt with later.)

Ninth   With all documentation in order and up to date (as outlined in Chapter 2).

Tenth   According to the conditions laid down in BPA Parachuting Regulations (given in Appendix A).

The final subject in this chapter is ground control organisation. This is important as without a systematic organisation the control of parachuting will become haphazard and possibly even dangerous. Of course, the responsibility of this organisation rests squarely on the shoulders of the Club Chief Instructor, and it will vary from club to club, but the following basic rules must apply:

First, all parachutists must be briefed and inspected before emplaning. The briefing of students will obviously take longer than the briefing of the more experienced jumpers. The student's briefing will be given individually first and then as a lift (or aircraft load) collectively by your instructor. You shouldn't have any queries at this late stage but if there is any little detail that you're not absolutely clear about you must ask. You will, of course, be inspected (or given a 'pin-check' as it's sometimes called) and details of this are covered in Chapter 18.

Secondly, all aircraft lifts must be correctly manifested before emplaning. This manifesting will not necessarily be completed by your instructor but may be done by an experienced parachutist or ground instructor who is known as the marshaller. It is best done by writing each lift by name only on a blackboard and drawing a line across it as it takes off. This will allow any parachutist to see at a glance when it is time for him to fit his equipment. Additionally, two copies of the manifest should be written and clipped to two separate mill boards. One mill board is kept by the marshaller and the second is used by the instructor in the aircraft. Normally a manifest sheet is made out as follows:

AIRCRAFT:		TIME OF FLIGHT:	
LIFT NO:		JUMPMASTER:	
NAME	TYPE OF JUMP	COST	REMARKS

Thirdly, DZ control must be continuously established when parachuting is in progress, and the descent of all parachutists must be observed from the ground. A DZ controller will be nominated from experienced parachutists and thoroughly briefed by the Club Chief Instructor, and he will be responsible for the control of the DZ until the last parachutist has landed. The DZ controller's recommended duties are given in a later chapter as it is not essential that you should know them at this stage. The DZ controller is responsible for laying out the target cross and you should know the basics of the system. The target cross is made up of fluorescent panels which can be seen from whatever height parachuting is taking place. When placed as a full cross it indicates that conditions are suitable for categories of parachutists and it also indicates the approximate centre of the DZ, or the target area in which you are expected to land. If the target cross is removed altogether it means that the DZ controller has decided that parachuting should be suspended (normally because of a change to adverse weather conditions) and if the aircraft is airborne, it should land immediately. If the cross is distorted to a 'T' it means that only those nominated by the Chief Instructor may jump and if it is distorted to an 'I' it means jumping is temporarily suspended until the target is changed to any of the other signals. The DZ controller should be equipped with some means of knowing the surface wind speed. Some clubs use their own anemometer while others rely on the instruments available in the flying club or control tower. All DZs should have a windsock which as you will find out later, is a very useful item of equipment.

Finally, after your descent you must be debriefed by your instructor.

Now while it is his duty to ensure that you are properly debriefed, it is partly up to you to make sure he does. When you land, don't rush off for a quick celebration or to give your girl friend a heart-throbbing account of your descent; get hold of your instructor while it's still fresh in your mind and ask him how you got on. He will be told how you performed, once your canopy had developed, by the DZ controller and this, together with what he saw, will enable him to go through your whole descent with you step by step. I must stress the vital importance of your being properly debriefed and if you aren't bothered about your performance then you're wasting your time. At some clubs you may find that in addition to an individual critique, all students (having completed a jump each) will be debriefed collectively by the Chief Instructor. This is an excellent idea as you can learn from the mistakes of others–it's also comforting to know that others make mistakes!

To conclude this chapter I will emphasise a point I made at the beginning. Although the sound, thorough and progressive training of the student by a competent instructor is the best insurance against mishap, a great deal depends on that student–YOU.

Chapter 5

Aircraft Drills

It is very easy to think of a parachute descent as being the time between leaving an aircraft in flight and landing under an expanse of nylon; but in sport parachuting the parachute descent might best be defined as being the time between fitting your equipment and taking it off again having landed.

Now, as much of this time is spent in an aircraft it is important that you know about parachuting aircraft and the drills used in them. It would be impossible for me to describe all the aircraft used for parachuting as the list is almost unending; however, it will help if we examine initially the sort of aircraft suitable for the sport and then look at a few specific types.

An aircraft suitable for parachuting should have a high rate of climb, low running and maintenance costs, the ability to fly stably at less than 80 knots, a door which can be removed (or opened) in flight and which allows a clear exit, and finally it must be approved for parachuting by the Civil Aviation Authority, (or in the case of service aircraft by A and AEE Boscombe Down). This narrows the field considerably and you should bear in mind that no one has yet developed an aircraft for the specific purpose of sport parachute flying–apart from one or two modified specially for the sport. Therefore, we've got to make do with aircraft types that are available. Very few clubs own their own parachuting aircraft (although one or two hire aircraft that are used for the sport alone), and the rest hire aircraft from the local flying club.

Of all aircraft types, the DH 89A Rapide has probably given the most trustworthy service to the sport. A twin-engined pre-war biplane, she has a suitability that is not easily rivalled. She can carry eight parachutists in comparative comfort, and the door's positioning by the roots of the lower wing affords the student parachutist a simple, uncluttered exit. The pilot has a single seat cabin but this does not hinder his communication with the jumpers. Some Rapides have a system of lights on the instrument panel with which to signal the pilot (these lights being operated by buttons or a multi-position switch by the door); others have a mirror whereby the pilot usually receives the signals from the jumpmaster and the rest rely on verbal communication. The jumpers normally sit two abreast on the floor, facing the rear of the aircraft while the jumpmaster sits in a seat by the door facing forwards. A word about jumpmasters at this stage is necessary. Until you reach Category VI your jumpmaster will always be an instructor. The jumpmaster is responsible for the briefing of the pilot, for taking charge of the remaining parachutists, for lining up the aircraft (spotting) and dispatching all the parachutists safely over the correct point on the ground.

Unfortunately, the faithful Rapide is gradually nearing the end of its useful life. Every year replacement engines are more difficult to obtain and maintenance generally becomes more costly. Mercifully in a few cases their life has been extended by converting them to different engines (Gipsy Queen IIs instead of Gipsy Sixes) with constant speed propellers.

Therefore it is becoming more likely that you will parachute from modern aircraft and the most popular of these is the Cessna 172 series. The

The Cessna 172 prepared for parachuting with the starboard door and wheel spats removed. The 172 is probably the World's most widely used sport parachuting aircraft

172 is a high-winged, single-engined monoplane which carries the pilot and three parachutists. One parachutist sits on the floor facing forwards next to the pilot and the other two sit abreast behind, also facing forwards. Movement is much more restricted than in the Rapide and it is important that you are aware of this as you will see shortly. Communication between parachutists and pilot can be verbal, visual (by signalling with one hand) or by using a system of taps on the pilot's shoulder.

The other modern aircraft you might well jump from is the Cherokee 6 series. This is a low-winged monoplane which can carry the pilot and six parachutists in relative comfort. The parachutists are positioned in the aircraft facing towards the rear, with the jumpmaster sitting by the door facing forwards (in much the same way as the Rapide but a lower cabin roof does not permit the same freedom of movement). The only disadvantage of this aircraft is the low wing, which makes spotting a little more difficult, but with practice you will not consider it as such. Other aircraft which you may come across and which are highly suitable for parachuting include the big brothers of the Cessna 172 series, the 180 series (4 parachutists), the 206 and 207 Skywagons (5 and 6 parachutists respectively), the twin-engined, high-winged Britten-Norman Islander (9 parachutists), and finally (and in my opinion the best of the lot), the Pilatus Turbo-Porter, which is a single-engined, turbo-propped aircraft with a high wing configuration, sliding doors and a capability of lifting eight parachutists at a very high rate of climb.

A word on parachuting (or jump) pilots at this stage seems appropriate. Good parachuting pilots are few and far between for a variety of different reasons. Firstly, flying for parachuting has to be precise and requires a number of techniques that are not normally employed in other types of flying. The pilot must fly up to jump height as fast as he can and once he has dropped his jumpers he must put the aircraft back on the ground as quickly as possible. He must reach the jump altitude exactly over the drop zone (unless he's been specifically briefed to give a climbing pass over the DZ), for if he has a mile or two run-in at jump height, he's wasting time. Constantly he should be made to understand that time means money and you're paying. Eventually he himself will come up with ideas for reducing flying time (and thus cost), e.g. having the fuel tanks only half full or using thermals to gain altitude faster. (If he's a pilot who's using parachutists only to increase the number of hours in his log book then he's not the type you want.) He must give you precise rudder turns on the run-ins. Normally a pilot turns an aircraft using an aileron (or banked) turn, which is a stable turn, but when spotting the jumpmaster has to be able to look straight down. A precise rudder turn made by the pilot using the rudder and a touch of opposite aileron takes a good deal of practice to perfect. All these things require a pilot to fly the aircraft all the time and when he starts he must accept that the techniques *are* different and *do* require practice. Often a really experienced pilot does not make a good jump pilot as he believes he knows it all and parachuting flying isn't really any different – in this connection airline pilots often make the worst jump pilots of all! Secondly, an aircraft can receive terrible treatment when used for parachuting. Constant fast climbs and descents can increase engine wear and maintenance, and the interiors of cabins can become very tatty by being knocked by bodies struggling for the door and the hardware on the harness catching on the carpeting and upholstery. Therefore, if the pilot has a material interest in the aircraft, the novelty of having it maltreated is liable to wear a little thin.

Finally, remember the human touch. It's very easy to be cynical and just regard your pilot as a glorified taxi-driver but, as I've said before, if you didn't have a pilot, you'd have considerable difficulty jumping – (if you didn't have a taxi-driver you could always go by bus or tube, or even walk!). Therefore, always give your pilot a willing hand to push out (or put away) the aircraft, and prepare it; offer him a cigarette or coffee every so often, and above all, at the end of the day say 'thank you'. (This all sounds very obvious but half the parachutists jumping today don't even know the name of their regular jump pilot!)

The preparation of an aircraft for parachuting is normally fairly simple and should be carried out with your pilot's help or advice. It usually consists of removing the seats, securing seat belts, removing unnecessary equipment and taping up any sharp objects, especially near or around the door.

Now we shall consider the actual drills used in the aircraft, both routine and in cases of emergency. Although the pilot of any aircraft is always in command of it and its passengers, and is responsible for them, the jumpmaster must accept direct responsibility for the conduct of the jumpers. This sounds a contradiction, but I hope by the end of the chapter you will see that it is not so, and that pilot and jumpmaster work as a team with the former being the ultimate boss.

Aircraft drills will be covered very thoroughly by your instructor on

Student George Hutchinson receiving exit training from Sport Parachute Centre Instructor Ronnie O'Brien

the ground, either by using a mock-up of the aircraft or the aircraft itself. The majority of parachuting aircraft have only just enough room to move around within their cabins and therefore from the beginning you should be constantly aware of the possibilities of catching pieces of your equipment either on other parachutists' equipment or on protrusions within the aircraft itself. The most dangerous of these possibilities is that of catching the reserve ripcord handle, thus releasing the pins and having the reserve canopy deploying within the aircraft. If this should happen and you spot it just as the canopy starts to appear, grab the whole reserve pack with both arms and clutch it to you firmly. If you are close to the open door, try to move away or turn your back towards it to prevent the slipstream tearing the canopy from your grip. If you are close to the door and the slipstream does catch hold of your reserve canopy and start to deploy it within the aircraft, you really have got a problem. If you just sit tight the inflation of the canopy in the slipstream will either pull in a straight line, probably through the side of the fuselage itself, or it will wrap itself around the tailplane with you on the end–it could even rip the tail fin or an elevator clean away, thus bringing the whole aircraft down. I don't wish to paint too grim a picture because if you are near the door and this situation does start to develop, there is no problem so long as you react quickly and correctly. As you see the canopy start to snake out of the door, you must dive out after it and the chances are that the jumpmaster will be assisting you with a tactically placed size 10 jump boot. (If you freeze, the chances are that he'll throw you out bodily, anyway!) Then all you can do is enjoy the ride back to earth under a slightly smaller canopy. It all sounds terrifying, but the point I am making here is that this situation need never arise if you protect your reserve handle with one hand and move carefully in the aircraft when you have to. If you feel any part of your equipment caught on anything, don't pull against it– just relax, find the cause, sort it out and start again. It'll be a lot quicker and safer in the long run.

Once all the parachutists in the aircraft are positioned correctly and the pilot briefed by the jumpmaster (this briefing will be dealt with in detail in Chapter 13), you're ready for take-off. As far as parachuting is concerned, the take-off is probably the most dodgy part. (Aircraft landings are no problem as parachutists don't often get involved with them!) The first thing to remember is that the pilot is flying with a full load and often fuel tanks topped right up; therefore you should keep still during take-off. Once the wheels leave the runway you're virtually helpless, if anything should go wrong with the aircraft, until you reach a safe *emergency* jumping height. As in all emergencies, it would be wrong to think that they happen on every flight but it would be foolish not to prepare for them. The most likely emergency on take-off is either partial or total engine failure. If this should occur, the only thing you can do is brace yourself for the inevitable hard landing, unless you have reached emergency jumping height. Now we have the problem 'What is emergency jumping height?'

It is difficult to lay down a hard and fast rule as a number of factors have to be taken into consideration. The first is the pilot who, on engine failure, will have plenty on his mind. He may well shout to the para-chutists to stay put because any rush to the door will obviously upset the trim of the aircraft, but if he says nothing it may well be up to the jumpmaster to make a decision (he can argue about the validity of this with the pilot when it's all over!).

The next consideration is the experience of the jumpers in the aircraft. The most inexperienced jumper is, naturally, the static line student. Normally the static line is not hooked up to the strong point (or cable if the aircraft has one) until the aircraft has reached a height of 1,000 feet above ground level, the reason being that the main parachute takes longer to deploy than the reserve (explained in Chapter 3) and if your static line were hooked up it would be your main that would open if you had to jump in an emergency. In some aircraft with restrictive interiors static lines have to be hooked up on the ground and the risk of having to use your main parachute at low altitude in an emergency must be accepted. Therefore it is generally agreed that in cases of aircraft difficulties the following is the rule: below 400 feet—sit tight and brace yourself for the aircraft crashing; 400–1,000 feet—exit the aircraft and use the reserve parachute; above 1,000 feet—exit the aircraft and use the main parachute. The first of these three alternatives is the sound obligatory reason for wearing your helmet during take-off! I have heard experienced parachutists say they would leave an aircraft in an emergency at 100 feet using a pilot 'chuted reserve, but remember that in your student days you will be in the hands of your instructor and he will usually make a decision which will be in line with the rule above. If the aircraft gets into difficulties between 400 feet and 1,000 feet and your static line has not been hooked up it is more than likely that your instructor will tell you to jump using your reserve. If this should be the case you should exit the aircraft as quickly as possible holding the reserve parachute ripcord handle in your right hand and, as soon as you are clear, pull the handle sharply away. The dangers of opening the parachute *before* you're clear of the aircraft have already been described. The final point to remember during aircraft emergencies is to watch your instructor for orders and, when you receive them, carry them out quickly and without panic. A real-life emergency that happened a couple of years ago might well help to illustrate some of the points I have been making. The Rapide, flown by a relatively inexperienced pilot, had reached about 700 feet with eight static line students and their instructor on board. The instructor suddenly spotted that the port engine cowling was starting to peel off and he immediately informed the pilot, who was already starting to notice some unusual handling characteristics (to say the least!) The pilot panicked slightly and informed everyone that he was going in to land. The instructor reasoned with him, as the proposed landing with a full load and an uncalled-for air brake on the port side looked like being interesting! The pilot calmed down and even managed to coax a few more feet out of the Rapide and line her up over the airfield; meanwhile, the instructor coolly hooked up the students, dispatched them and jumped out after them. They all landed safely on the airfield, followed soon after by the aircraft flown by a somewhat wiser pilot. The lessons here are obvious:

    (*a*)   Learn all aircraft emergency procedures as a drill.

    (*b*)   If an emergency occurs, keep calm and

    (*c*)   carry out the drills as practised.

Any instructions given in the aircraft, such as moving into a kneeling position or moving towards the door, should always be given by visual signals learnt beforehand. As a student you will have quite enough to think about without having to interpret the instructor's verbal directions given in competition with the noise of the aircraft engines.

Once you have reached 1,000 feet and have had your static line hooked to the strong point by your instructor, it is a good idea to hold the static line in one hand so you have control of it when moving in the aircraft. If the aircraft lurches, however, make sure you take any strain on the static line at the strong point end! The final check by your instructor before exit is that of making sure that the static line is running clear from the strong point to the top of your pack and therefore that any control you have of it will assist him considerably.

It is not practical to detail the exact moves that have to be made within the aircraft as they vary so considerably, from type to type, but your instructor will go through them with you very thoroughly, showing the exact positions of your hands and feet at any given moment. These 'drills' will be practised until they become automatic, so that before your first descent your movements within the aircraft are lively and precise.

Having reached the door, you then have the problem of the exit itself and this is the subject of the following chapter.

Chapter 6

The Exit and the Stable Position

The correct exit is that which enables the student to attain the stable position at the instant of parting company with the aircraft. It therefore seems logical to discuss the stable position and its importance before examining how to achieve it by a correct exit. When the parachute opens, activated by either static line or ripcord, it is essential that the parachutist is in such a position that the parachute is free to develop directly away from his body. With the main parachute mounted on his back, this body position must be such that the parachutist has his back uppermost and his stomach towards the earth. If this position were reversed the parachutist would be turned round violently upon canopy deployment with a danger of parts of the parachute being entangled with his extended limbs. To attain the correct opening position you will initially be taught the basic 'full spread' stable position. Study this position as illustrated in Figure 6a carefully. You will see that the basis is a well arched back combined with extended arms and legs. The head is forced back, with the back of the helmet against the top of the back pack and eyes on the horizon. The arms are spread out to each side of the body and in line with the shoulders while the legs are spread at an angle of about 45 degrees, level with each other and slightly bent at the knees. If the arms are positioned too far forward it could cause the head to rise up and a twisting of the body in free fall through a longitudinal axis, while if the arms are allowed to come too far back, the head will tend to drop. Any bending of the arms or legs asymmetrically may cause the body to turn around a vertical axis, or at worst uncontrolled tumbling. Now why should this position (correctly performed) make you fall stomach downwards and allow the parachute to deploy directly away from your body? A simple analogy here may be of assistance. If you were to take a saucer, the right way up, and sink it in a large tank of water, it would gently sink with its base towards the bottom of the tank. If, however, you were to place it upside down in the tank and let it sink, it would immediately turn over and float to the bottom the right way up. Another way to illustrate this is to cut out of a piece of card the approximate silhouette of a parachutist in the full spread position as shown in Figure 6b, then bend it to the position shown in Figure 6a. If you now hold your model skydiver against the ceiling

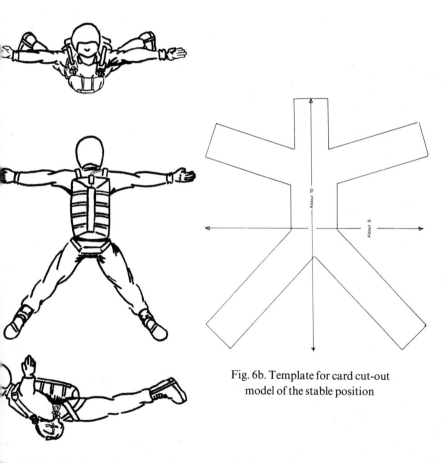

Fig. 6b. Template for card cut-out
model of the stable position

Fig. 6a. The full spread stable position

the right way up and drop him, he will 'free fall' to the floor remaining
the right way up. If you then repeat the operation, this time dropping
him upside down, you will see him turn over and land the right way up.
You will find it very exhilarating to prove this practically later on in
your progression when you are taught to dive out of the door, let yourself tumble for a few seconds, then arch sharply into the stable position –
instantly you will turn over and find yourself in the basic face to earth
position . . . but more of this later.

It is important that you practise this position and this is easily done at
home. Firstly, remove any aged relatives from the living-room, then
lie face downwards with your arms and legs extended and relaxed on
the floor. On the mental word of command to yourself of 'GO!' force
yourself into the position illustrated in Figure 6a. Your head should be
thrown up and your back arched vigorously so that you are looking at
a point about two-thirds of the way up the wall facing you. Your legs
and arms should also be completely clear of the floor. If you do it
correctly this position will be very uncomfortable after about 20
seconds and it does wonders for your stomach muscles! You should go
on practising the full spread position in this way until it is completely
second nature.

You can now see that the exit should be designed to enable you to
attain the stable position as quickly and simply as possible. The exit
you will use initially is therefore called the 'poised' or 'stable' exit.

John Noakes of BBC Children's TV 'Blue Peter' demonstrates a forceful
stable exit at the start of the ten-second delay

The stable exit will vary in detail from aircraft type to aircraft type but the general principle is that upon receiving the necessary hand signal from your instructor you move to the poised position either on the sill of the door or on a step outside the door. Here you pause momentarily, look in at your instructor, who taps you on the leg and shouts 'GO!' which is your signal to thrust yourself into the stable position as you leave the aircraft. It would be as well here to look in detail at three specific aircraft types, which should give you enough basic detail for just about any aircraft type.

The easiest of the three is undoubtedly the Rapide exit. Initially you will be crouching by the door and facing it. When your instructor points to the door, pull yourself up with your right hand using the pillar between the forward edge of the door and the window just in front of it. Then reach outside with your left hand for the strut which goes from the upper wing root diagonally down to the engine cowling. Follow this with your left foot which you place on the step with the toe forward and the heel just over the trailing edge of the wing. Now you pull yourself out on to the wing completely, placing the right hand alongside the left, gripping the strut, and the right foot next to the left. As in all aircraft the first thing of which you will immediately be aware is the 'slipstream' (or windblast)–remember you will be stepping from the relative calm of the cabin on to the wing, where the airflow is about 70 m.p.h. The pilot will have slowed the aircraft considerably before your exit but unless you are prepared for it, the slipstream effect may tend to throw you off your balance. In fact this slipstream shouldn't bother you as now you are well aware of its presence. Once you are comfortably positioned on the wing, look in at your instructor; this will show him that you are ready for the 'off' He will tap you on the leg and shout the magic word 'GO!' You should then make a small hop backwards and instantaneously thrust yourself into the stable position already described. I personally believe the secret to achieving the correct position is to throw your head sharply back and look up at the aircraft as you fall away from it. If you see your instructor watching you from the door, it is likely that you are in the correct position. This principle holds good for poised exits from all types of aircraft.

The Cessna-type exit is very similar to the Rapide's. The essential differences are that the door is on the starboard side of the aircraft as opposed to the port side of the Rapide, and that you will have to poise yourself for exit on the step and wheel instead of the latter's convenient lower mainplane. When your instructor points to the door, place your left foot on the step and reach out for the mainplane strut with your left hand. Now pull yourself out of the door and, turning forwards, place your right foot on the wheel (the pilot will have been told to apply the brakes if he doesn't already know the form; the sight of a student doing a treadmill act on the wheel is very amusing to all but the student!). Some Cessnas have a small platform specially built over the wheel which is used to simplify this type of exit. Finally, your right hand is placed about a foot to the right of the left hand on the strut. I believe it is easiest for you to have alternate grips with your hands, i.e. one an overhand grip–the other underhand; and this should apply to all aircraft where you have to hold on to a strut. You're now poised for the exit and once again you should look at your instructor for his signal to 'GO!' From here it is exactly the same as previously described for the Rapide. (See Figure 7).

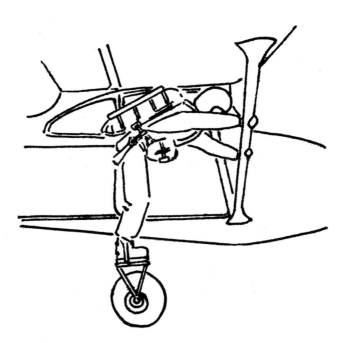

Fig. 7. A poised exit from a Cessna 172

The most tricky poised exit is that used in aircraft which have no step on which to poise for the exit. The Cherokee Six is an example of this. When your instructor points towards the door you should move into a sitting position on the sill with your legs dangling outside the aircraft. If the door is on the port side of the aircraft you should hold on to the upper end of the door frame with your right hand, and your left hand should be curled around the sill by your left thigh. Again the magic word 'GO!' but this time you must pivot forwards facing the slipstream as you exit. To do this you should pull with your right and push off with your left. Your left hand should reach out as far as possible as you pivot the rest of your body over the sill into the stable position as before. If the door is on the starboard side, the procedure is obviously exactly the opposite to that just described. This particular exit will require more practice than the other two, and exit practice can also be carried out at home, although it is best to use an accurate mock-up of the aircraft if possible.

The first two exits may be practised by standing in the poised, semi-crouched position on a low stool or bench, with your arms in front of you gripping an imaginary strut. On giving yourself the mental command 'GO!', jump backwards, thrusting yourself into the stable position. You should now be standing on the floor with your feet about 3 feet apart, your back arched, your arms outstretched and your head thrown back so you are looking up at the ceiling. If you want to be really vigorous with this one it's a good idea to have a friend standing behind to catch you, otherwise you're liable to hurl yourself through the television set! To practise the third exit, it's best to use a solid table as the sill of the aircraft and have a friend holding vertically a broom or the like as a substitute for the door frame. The drill can then be practised as originally described, finishing with your standing on the floor in the stable position (described above).

Throughout this chapter I have referred to the use of the command 'GO!'. Naturally, when it's time to 'GO!' on your first descent you will have your fair share of anxiety; this is nothing to worry about, in fact it's perfectly normal. However, it's essential that you do react instantaneously to the command of 'GO!' and to this end your instructor will use it constantly throughout your training; on practising parachute landings and exit drills, and even when moving from one lesson to the next. When, therefore, the ultimate real 'GO!' arrives, you react without giving it a second thought.

The final subject to be covered in this chapter is the verbal count. This is very important and gives a direct lead into the next chapter on emergency procedures. The verbal count is a vital aid to being aware of the number of seconds your parachute is taking to deploy. A second is very accurately accounted for verbally by saying 'one thousand' at your normal speaking rate. I shall only show you its use for static line descents in this chapter and the verbal count for free fall descents will be covered in Chapter 11. For the static line assisted deployment the verbal count is four seconds. So on the word of command 'GO!' you launch yourself into the stable position and immediately start the verbal count by SHOUTING OUT LOUD (loud enough for the pilot to hear!) 'One thousand, two thousand, three thousand, four thousand, check!' On the word 'check' you look sharply over your shoulder and check that the canopy is deploying satisfactorily. Whatever the count (and it may vary slightly from club to club), your instructor will go through it very thoroughly. The verbal count, however, is something you can practise yourself in conjunction with all the exercises described earlier in this chapter; so when you give yourself the command of 'GO!' shout out the count, at the same time going through the motions described. Hold the necessary position until you finish the count . . . then relax. Make sure you actually shout out the count, (this will confirm your elderly relatives' views on your lack of sanity!); if you get into the habit of just saying it to yourself then you'll surely forget to count at all when you actually carry out a live descent. You will see the importance of the verbal count in the following chapter.

Chapter 7

Emergency Procedures

If there is one chapter in this book that you should read again and again and again . . . then this is it! The key word in the conduct of the sport of parachuting is SAFETY and therefore your ability to deal with any out of the ordinary situation is of paramount importance. This chapter deals with parachute malfunctions and the procedures (to be carried out as drills) to be employed in each case to give you a safe landing. Your first reaction after reading this chapter could be a terrified awakening to the number of things that could go wrong, but I would, however, like it to be one of confidence in your ability to cope with these emergency situations. Let us, therefore, view these potential emergencies in perspective. I personally know jumpers with over a thousand descents who've never had any kind of parachute malfunction; and at the other end of the scale I know one stalwart operator who landed on his reserve parachute twice running! Parachute malfunctions rarely occur but the drills for coping with them are taught to you really thoroughly so that you can put them to immediate good use if necessary.

Parachute malfunctions are normally caused by one (or a combination) of the following: faulty equipment, bad parachute packing or a poor body position during canopy deployment. Faulty equipment is less and less liable to contribute to a parachute malfunction as the standard of sport parachute equipment is improving all the time. Gone are the pioneer days when jumpers were equipped with parachutes of extremely doubtful origins and varying states of air-worthiness. Initially you are likely to use well-maintained club equipment and a point worth making at this stage is that if you decide to buy your own, make sure you have your Chief Instructor check it out thoroughly before you part with the cash. Bad parachute packing is unlikely to cause a malfunction during your student days for two reasons: first, when you initially start packing your own parachute it's quite extraordinary how meticulous you will be! and, secondly, until you are granted a packing certificate, an instructor will carefully check each stage of your packing. However, once you are qualified to pack your own parachute there is a tendency to become lax and you may start to listen to the more irresponsible brethren when they say 'It only takes me five minutes to pack the old rag . . . and it always opens.' Don't you believe it! I am certain that careless packing is responsible for more malfunctions than these so-called experts care to admit. Thirdly, a poor body position during canopy deployment is the most likely cause of a malfunction during your early descents, and that is why the previous chapter is so important. Having examined the most likely causes of parachute malfunctions I shall now discuss your biggest enemy in the unlikely event of your having a malfunction–TIME. Experience and the possibility of a malfunction have produced an opening height for the main parachute of between 2,200 feet (minimum) and 2,500 feet–on static line descents you will not drop from less than 2,500 feet. Therefore, with no parachute and falling at terminal velocity of 120 m.p.h. (176 feet per second) it would take you between 12 and 14 seconds to reach the ground. This means that, in the worst case of a total malfunction (complete non-appearance of the parachute) and allowing for your reaction time, carrying out the drill as taught and your reserve parachute deploying, you should be safely suspended under your reserve well above 1,000 feet. Any partial malfunction (i.e. part of the canopy deployed) will slow your rate of descent and give you more time to sort out the problem.

Following on from the last chapter we return to the verbal count. Once you have exited the aircraft (on a static line descent) and have reached the end of the count at the word 'check', you look sharply over your shoulder to check that your parachute is deploying correctly. Now if your verbal count has not been gabbled (the most usual tendency) and has taken the correct time, you will find that by the time you shouted 'check' you will already have been pulled into a vertical position by the deploying parachute which will be billowing out above you. All you will have to do is watch the canopy fill out completely with air if it hasn't done so already. This, therefore, is the picture assuming that the parachute deploys normally. If, however, when you shout 'check', you look over your shoulder and see nothing, you may have encountered a malfunction.

Before describing the types of malfunction that may be encountered, it is important to cover the standard reserve deployment drill, which you'll be practising constantly during your training until it becomes automatic.

LOOK FOR THE RESERVE HANDLE—GRASP FIRMLY WITH THE RIGHT HAND—PLACE THE LEFT HAND ROUND THE FRONT OF THE RESERVE CONTAINER—FEET TOGETHER—PULL THE HANDLE AND THROW IT AWAY—GRAB THE RESERVE CANOPY WITH BOTH HANDS AND THROW IT HARD, DOWN AND AWAY FROM YOU. (This procedure is illustrated in figure 8.)

This procedure is good for all malfunctions in your student days, but may be modified when you have gained Category VIII as we will discuss later.

The first malfunction is the pilot 'chute hesitation.

The pilot 'chute hesitation or 'burble' is caused by one of two things: either your body position on canopy deployment is such that it accentuates the low pressure area (or partial vacuum) in the small of your back caused by your passage through the air, or the coiled spring in your pilot 'chute may be too weak. In the first case it is possible that your pilot 'chute leaves the pack tray but bobs around in the low pressure area and is unable to be deployed by slipstream of your body. In the second case, the weakened spring simply hasn't got enough 'oomph' to push the pilot 'chute into your body's slipstream. Regular maintenance of your equipment will prevent the second possibility and the static line assisted deployment (the end of the static line being attached to the loop at the base of the pilot 'chute by break cord or Velcro tape ... remember?) will obviate the possibility of a pilot 'chute hesitation altogether. However, the eventuality could arise when you progress to free fall descents; therefore you must know the cure. On the 'check' you may or may not even observe the pilot 'chute bobbing around in the small of your back, but you should carry out the reserve procedure immediately. If this is done correctly it will have the effect of turning you over and allowing the direct airflow past your body to 'catch' the pilot 'chute and thus deploy the main canopy in the normal way, possibly even before you have chance to pull the handle. But the drill during your first few descents must be to pull the reserve handle right away, although we must accept the possibility of the main and reserve deploying together. After a few descents it will be expected that you could either pause for a second with your right hand on the handle, to see if the main does deploy as explained above, or you could eliminate the low pressure area by dipping one shoulder and thus allowing the slipstream to grab the pilot 'chute.

The next possible malfunction is the least likely; it is the total malfunction. In this case the count has been completed and nothing has appeared at all. It could be caused (on static line rigs) by the failure to remove temporary packing pins (which are now totally banned– more of this in Chapter 10). It could be caused by bent ripcord pins (if you are on a free fall descent) . . . and so on, but you can analyse the cause later. Of possible malfunctions this one is the easiest with which to deal because there is no partly deployed canopy to interfere with the deployment of the reserve. Don't delay–pull your reserve handle right away. The important thing to remember while you practise this drill is that, although it is the easiest malfunction to rectify, you will have the least time in which to carry it out. During your first few descents you will not be able to differentiate between the pilot 'chute hesitation and the total malfunction; don't let this worry you, just react immediately and deploy your reserve.

The 'streamer' malfunction is an unusual one whereby the rigging lines deploy, pulling you into an upright position, but the canopy does not inflate (either the sleeve fails to slide off or the lower peripheral band simply does not open out). The resultant drag will decrease your rate of descent very slightly but here again you must react quickly. Do not try and shake the main open but go straight in for the reserve. As you pull the handle keep both hands spread in front of you to prevent the reserve going straight up into the main.

The most controversial malfunction is the partial malfunction which can vary from being stable to spinning violently or from a division of the canopy into two brassiere-shaped lobes (the Mae West), to a canopy which is badly torn. I say controversial as it is only recently that the majority of experts have agreed on the various procedures. If you are taught any different procedures from those outlined below make sure your instructor can justify them. Basically there are two methods of deploying the reserve parachute should you experience a partial malfunction. The first is to deploy the reserve with the partial malfunction still flying above you and the second is to 'cutaway'. The cutaway system is when you jettison the main parachute altogether by means of the Capewell releases and then deploy the reserve. In your student days, however, this latter system should definitely NOT be used and until you have gained Category VIII, the first system is the safer if practised until it becomes automatic. The second system, of the 'cutaway', is the safer, however, when you start to jump with high performance canopies, having gained Category VIII, and your instructor would be unwise to grant you Category VIII for this very reason.

Now we come to the thorny problem of whether to jump with a pilot 'chute in the reserve parachute, or not.

A pilot 'chute in the reserve parachute will obviously cause the reserve canopy to deploy very quickly, especially in the case of a total malfunction or cutaway; but the disadvantage of this system is that if a pilot 'chuted reserve is deployed under a rotating or spinning malfunction, there is a very real danger of losing control and having it 'barber-pole' around the partial malfunction. The advantage of not having a pilot 'chute in the reserve parachute is that you will have more control of the reserve canopy should you be forced to deploy it while you still have a partial malfunction flying above you. Therefore, the teaching should be as follows: until you have gained Category VIII and are jumping a sophisticated sport parachute you should *not* have a pilot 'chute in the reserve and should not, therefore, cutaway in the event of a partial malfunction. However, once you have Category VIII and when you start jumping high-performance sport parachutes, you should never deploy a reserve under a partial malfunction, as it will almost certainly be rotating: you should cutaway and, therefore, you must have a pilot 'chute in the reserve parachute.

Many will argue that having no pilot 'chute in the reserve is a dangerous practice in the case of a total malfunction but they have little case, for, if you are taught your emergency procedures correctly, you will still have plenty of time to deploy your reserve; the addition of a pilot 'chute in the reserve only speeds up the opening of the reserve by about 100–150 feet anyway.

The easiest partial malfunctions you may encounter are the stable type which could be broken lines, torn canopy or the stable Mae West, or any combination of the three. There is no way to cure the first two possibilities, but the third is slightly different. The 'Mae West' malfunction is easily recognised as the canopy has become divided into two or more lobes on deployment by rigging lines caught over the top of the canopy or by the peripheral hem blown back over the canopy to cause a similar condition. If your rate of descent is not too great–

other jumpers in the sky will give you a guide—you can spend a *short* time trying to clear the Mae West (sometimes called the 'thrown line' or 'blown periphery' (BP)), by pulling down sharply on the lines which appear to be causing it. If after this short time the malfunction is still apparent, you must deal with it in the same way as previously taught. The reserve should inflate, but if the main is giving you plenty of support it may well just flop down by your legs; don't worry—this is a sign that the malfunction isn't a desperate one and you have time to pull the reserve canopy in and attempt to fly it again. If the malfunction is serious, the reserve canopy will virtually deploy on its own, but you should be careful it does not tangle with the main as it goes up. Once the two canopies are flying it is a good idea to rest your forearms on the reserve rigging lines to try to keep it clear of the main. The seriously malfunctioned main will probably collapse completely after full deployment of the reserve and in this case it is a good idea to jettison the remnants of the main using the Capewell releases, or haul it in and hold the bundle between your legs to get it out of the way until you land. As you become more experienced a slight variation may be added: as the canopy starts to appear from the pack hold it firmly with the left hand and slide the right hand under the canopy and grasp the peripheral hem. Now throw it outwards as described above and in doing so grab the peripheral hem with the left hand, about two feet from the right hand. By shaking the canopy like a blanket with both hands, the deployment is speeded up but when using this refinement it is important that the reserve is packed with the peripheral hem on the right hand side.

The spinning or rotating malfunction, which is caused by an asymmetrical condition of the canopy, needs to be dealt with carefully when deploying a non-pilot 'chuted reserve while the main is still flying because of the danger of entanglement. Sometimes it is possible to slow or even stop the spinning by pulling down the steering toggle on the opposite side of the spin while the reserve is deployed. Beware of this, however, as any rotation quickly gathers speed, making your reserve deployment more hazardous. Quickly take the decision to deploy your reserve and carry out the procedures already described.

Let us proceed. You have Category VIII and have progressed to using a high-performance canopy. You now have a pilot 'chute in your reserve. It is important that you use an unattached 'kicker plate' under your reserve pilot 'chute. The 'kicker plate' is a light aluminium disc about six inches in diameter and its function is to provide a plat-

RESERVE DEPLOYMENT DRILL

Fig. 8. Reserve deployment drill

form from which the pilot 'chute can 'kick off'. If the plate is attached (or threaded by the bridle line) there is a danger of it becoming entangled with the canopy on deployment. The next requirement is that the harness should be fitted with suitable canopy releases. The various types of Capewell canopy releases have been described in Chapter 3. The old '2-shot' type is not suitable as they are awkward to operate, especially when wearing gloves. Of the '1½-shot' and '1-shot' I prefer the former because of the slight danger of accidently opening the latter. The '1½-shot' with its wire loop provides a positive and safe canopy release. Having fitted the pilot 'chute to your reserve you are now committed to cutting away in the event of a partial malfunction. If you have a partial malfunction on a high performance canopy, it is more than likely it will be rotating. The rotations will build up in speed very quickly, resulting in a high rate of descent; therefore it is imperative you react quickly by cutting away.

The cutaway procedure is straightforward. On checking the canopy and discovering the malfunction it is acceptable to spend a few seconds trying to clear it providing you are still above 2,000 feet. Once you are below 2,000 feet you are committed to cutting away in order to have the reserve flying by 1,700 feet at the lowest. Having made the decision DO NOT HESITATE. First, get rid of the main ripcord handle; secondly, adopt the position to ensure a back-to-earth position when you cut away – round your back and shoulders, and spread your legs in front of you. Thirdly, check the position of the reserve handle; fourthly, undo the protective covers of the Capewell, unless you're using '1-shot', in which case you should wait until after the fifth point, which is to check that there is no one immediately beneath you. Sixthly, put your thumbs through the wire loops of the '1½-shots' and pull them down sharply together. IMMEDIATELY you are free of the main pull the reserve handle – do not try and get stable. Finally, of course, check the reserve. When you have attained the experience of using the cutaway system you may feel it slightly beneath you to practise it on the ground – nonsense! Make sure you practise it thoroughly because the whole drill from the decision to reserve canopy deployment should take no more than five seconds.

If you are using a 'piggyback' rig the procedure is slightly different. The most important point here is that if it is manufactured with a static line system for reserve deployment DO NOT disconnect it; it is a proven life saver and you should not be tempted to modify it in any way.

On deciding to cutaway you should arch your back and bend your legs behind you so you are in a face-to-earth position when the reserve deploys. When you actually release the Capewells operate the right hand side just before the left to prevent the reserve deploying before the main is completely jettisoned.

An additional refinement with the piggyback system is to pull the reserve ripcord after the main is jettisoned, in addition to the static line doing its job...just in case!

Having run through these procedures for you I must again stress that they are worthless until you practise them so much that they become automatic drills. The best way of doing this is in the 'suspended harness'. If your club does not have one, they are easily rigged up using an old harness and pair of risers, the latter being suspended from the ceiling using 1000 lb. nylon cord.

Tears in canopies and an odd broken line do not necessarily require automatic use of the reserve parachute but remember that the decision to use the reserve parachute is entirely yours and the maxim here must obviously be 'If in doubt – get it out'.

Having carried out about a hundred descents and not having had to use the reserve parachute you may easily become complacent about it; regarding it as just a convenient place to mount your instruments and tossing it with gay abandon into the filthy boot of your car after a day's jumping. NEVER allow this state of mind to come about. Always treat your reserve parachute with a great deal of respect, take infinite care packing it (regularly) and don't throw it around. You never know when you may need it.

A word on reserve canopies is relevant. The following table has been recommended as being the safest guide for the varying weights of parachutists (without equipment):

Weight of Parachutist	Minimum Standard of Reserve Canopy
Up to 150 lbs	24 ft
150–175 lbs	26 ft conical (1.1 porosity nylon)
175–200 lbs	Lo-Po 26 ft conical or 28 ft 1.1 porosity nylon
Over 200 lbs	Lo-Po 28 ft or zero porosity tri-conical

Disregard for these standards could result in a fairly high rate of descent, which may (or may not) be acceptable in an emergency and which may cause minor injury. If in doubt, be guided by your instructor. As you gain experience you may realise the need for a steerable reserve, especially when jumping on to restricted DZs on displays; but don't be tempted to have any canopy modified unless expert advice is received from a qualified rigger. Most modern reserve canopies designed specifically for the sport are steerable and some have such an opening shock that it is best if they are used in a piggyback or mounted using longer risers which support you from the shoulders; however, the manufacturers will supply any of this type of information.

Another emergency of a slightly different nature needs to be dealt with in this chapter: the 'hang up'. The 'hang up' is when a static line student exits the aircraft and becomes suspended beneath it by his static line. It is exceptionally rare and if it does occur it will probably have been caused by a poor body position on exit and the static line not being properly controlled by the instructor; in fact the static line becomes entangled around a limb or equipment and this prevents it opening the pack, leaving the student dangling under the aircraft. It's a tricky state of affairs and, of course, the smaller the aircraft, the more difficult it will be for the pilot to remain in control. However, the procedure is simple. If you are conscious and in control of your faculties, you signal this to your instructor by placing both hands on your helmet. The instructor will then show you a knife which will indicate that he is going to cut you free. He won't cut you free, however, until you have grasped the reserve ripcord handle firmly with the right hand. DO NOT pull it until your instructor has cut through the static line because of the danger of the reserve deploying while you are still attached – if this occurred you'd more than likely cause the aircraft to crash. So, the instant you are cut free, pull the reserve handle violently and throw it away. Now relax and enjoy the safe ride to ground. If you are NOT in control of your faculties, all you need to know at this stage is that your instructor will shin down the static line, cut you free and deploy your reserve for you – he will make a normal free fall descent having done so. A hang up has happened only once in sport parachuting in Great Britain and the instructor was awarded the George Medal for successfully carrying out the second procedure described. But in spite of its rarity, the hang up and how to deal with it will be taught to you in detail.

I return here to automatic opening devices as you may find yourself using one during your first few descents. The first of the most proven AODs is the KAP 3, which is normally used in the main parachute. It is of Czechoslovakian manufacture and is used extensively in the Iron Curtain countries. The cable which actually pulls the ripcord is fired by a powerful spring, fired either barometrically or by a time system. It is rugged in construction and very reliable. One word of caution is necessary, however: when the KAP 3 is to be used barometrically it is important that care is taken to set the correct barometric pressure as described in the instructions which come with it. The second AOD, which has gained in usage in the USA where it was produced, is the Sentinel. This system has been designed for use with the reserve parachute and comes with a comprehensive handbook on its use and maintenance. The reserve pins are fired ballistically when a detonator is triggered barometrically at 1,000 feet. There is a simple adjustment to calibrate for changes in barometric pressure. Once the main parachute has been deployed successfully, it is necessary to switch off the Sentinel, otherwise the reserve will be deployed at 1,000 feet whether you like it or not! A recent development, however, prevents this eventuality; the Sentry auxiliary device automatically de-activates the Sentinel when the parachutist has decellerated to a rate of descent which is comparable to his flying under a correctly deployed main canopy.

Both systems need careful handling and both allow the ripcord handles to be deployed manually, thus overriding their use. As they are mechanical the possibility of their failure, however remote, should not be overlooked. But as their use should only be a back-up to all procedures described in this chapter, it is fair to say that their use can be a valid contribution to the safety of sport parachuting.

Now, what about the accidental deployment of the reserve parachute after leaving the aircraft? The most common causes of this are the student pulling the reserve handle instead of the dummy main ripcord handle during later static line descents, and the opening of the reserve when a pilot 'chute hesitation occurs. If the main and reserve are deploying together there is a danger of the two entangling; it may be that there is little you can do as·their deployment is so quick, but the action of keeping your arms out in front of you may help to keep the reserve away from the main. Once the two canopies are properly inflated there is little likelihood of any entanglement, but the alternative to continuing the descent under two canopies is to haul down the reserve and tuck it between your legs. (Your canopy control is very restricted with two canopies flying.) If the main is already inflated when you accidentally open the reserve, then you've no problems. Just gather up the reserve in a bundle and tuck it between your legs, gripping it firmly until after you've landed.

Finally, and with no apologies for repeating myself, remember that, although you may never need to use the reserve parachute, only correct teaching and constant practice will ensure that, should the necessity arise, you will carry out the emergency procedures with absolute confidence. The motto of No. 1 Parachute Training School, RAF, is 'Knowledge dispels Fear'; make sure you have this knowledge, theoretically and practically.

John Nickolls
Flying a reserve that probably was not necessary in this case

Chapter 8

Wind Determination and Canopy Control

The actual parachute descent under a fully deployed canopy can be divided into three distinct phases. First is the checking of the canopy and orientation; second is the steering of the canopy to land you in the target area, and finally, preparation for the landing itself. But before examining these parts of the descent in detail, it is necessary to look at the factors that effect both your vertical rate of descent and horizontal velocity across the ground. The first factor is your own weight; obviously the heavier you are, the faster you will come down! Your weight has a direct influence on the next factor, which is the overall performance of your parachute canopy: its rate of descent and inherent forward speed. Generally speaking, these two factors remain constant but the other factors are variables which are governed by the natural elements in which we live. The higher your DZ is above sea level, the greater your rate of descent due to the thinning of the atmosphere; actually, this increase in your rate of descent is relatively insignificant and will not affect you as much as the type of ground over which you will pass during your descent. The reason for this is that certain types of ground will absorb heat quicker than others and the resultant warmth will decrease your rate of descent should you pass through it. Woods and ploughs are examples, but the one you are most likely to encounter is tarmac or concrete when you pass over runways on airfields. On a warm summer day it is not uncommon to feel your rate of descent decrease to practically nothing when passing over a runway. The most relevant variable, however, is the wind.

On taking up parachuting, you will almost certainly take more of an interest in the wind and its varying moods than you ever thought possible. Wind will affect you in parachuting in two ways: speed and direction. Wind speed is normally measured in miles per hour, but it is important to think of wind speed in metres per second because of our immanent switch to metric. The following table gives you the comparison between m.p.h. and metres per second.

WIND SPEED CONVERSION TABLE

METRES PER SEC	M.P.H.	LIMITATIONS
1	2·25	
2	4·5	
3	6·75	UPPER LIMIT FOR STUDENTS (CATEGORIES I–V)
4	9	4·5 metres/sec or 10 m.p.h.
5	11·25	UPPER LIMIT FOR CATEGORIES VI–IX
6	13·5	6·5 metres/sec or 15 m.p.h.
7	15·75	UPPER LIMIT FOR CATEGORY X
8	18	8 metres/sec or 18 m.p.h.

Every club should be equipped with an accurate means of measuring the wind speed, and more often than not this will be an anemometer used by the normal air-traffic control organisation on the airfield. In early days you only need to know the wind speed before you jump to discover whether you are actually within the upper limit shown above. But the more experienced you become, the more important it will be for you to learn the ground wind speed in assisting the accuracy of your descent to the target.

Wind direction, however, is significant to you from your first descent onwards. Before you jump you should note the direction of the wind and on an airfield, the most usual aid is the windsock itself. (Not only will the windsock show you the direction of the wind but it will also give you indication of wind speed by its flying angle from the pole.) Flags, smoke (factory chimneys, stubble burning, etc.), washing on lines and the movement of clouds or foliage also give the visually alert parachutist aids to discovering wind direction, not only when he's standing on the airfield before his jump, but also when he's suspended beneath a fully-deployed canopy. Later you will discover the effect of upper winds (those above 2,500 feet) during longer free fall delays, but at this stage only the lower winds (those below 2,500 feet) are of direct consequence.

Obviously, to ensure that you land in the correct part of the airfield, it is important that your instructor despatches you over the correct point on the ground.

The whole business of spotting is explained in Chapter 13, but at this point it is relevant to mention the Wind Drift Indicator (WDI or 'streamer'). The Wind Drift Indicator is a strip of brightly coloured crepe paper, 20 feet long and ten inches wide, with a ten-inch rod weight taped across one end. When rolled up it should weigh about $3-3\frac{1}{2}$ ounces; this will cause it to descend, having unrolled after being thrown from the aircraft, at a speed which approximates to a parachutist's rate of descent under an inflated canopy. The WDI, therefore, gives an accurate assessment of lower wind speed and direction to enable your instructor to decide over what point on the ground he will dispatch you. Its precise use will be explained in Chapter 13 but you should know that a WDI must be dropped (*a*) before parachuting begins; (*b*) following a significant change in wind velocity or direction; (*c*) following a break in parachuting of more than 30 minutes caused by increase of wind in excess of the limits laid down in the table above, or (*d*) after parachutists have failed to land in the intended target area and a faulty 'spot' is not suspected.

Before you emplane, your instructor will show you the 'opening point', which is that point on the ground over which you should be positioned at the moment your canopy deploys. Of course, it will be your instructor's responsibility to dispatch you from the aircraft over the opening point. This may sound difficult but you should bear in mind that the opening point is not a precise point, but a fairly large area, as you will discover later in this chapter and in Chapter 13.

Your first thirty to fifty descents will more than likely be made using a 'double L' modification in a 28-foot circular canopy, and you should be thoroughly familiar with its inherent performance and how to control it before your first descent. Every parachute canopy has a trapped volume of air pressure inside it when inflated and all parachute canopies are manoeuvred by the control of this air pressure. This air pressure is initially directed in the design and manufacture of the canopy, and ultimately by your further control of this design when you're flying beneath it. All modified canopies have gores and 'steering windows' cut from the rear of the canopy and Figure 9 shows the

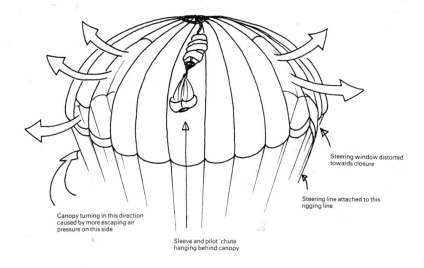

Steering window distorted
towards closure

Steering line attached to this
rigging line

Canopy turning in this direction
caused by more escaping air
pressure on this side

Sleeve and pilot chute
hanging behind canopy

Fig. 9. A 'double L' canopy undergoing a right turn

'double L' modification in some detail.

Therefore, you can see that when you are suspended beneath the inflated canopy, the built-up air pressure is permitted to 'escape' through the blank gores and steering windows at the back of it. This escaping air pressure, in fact, acts as two jets which push the canopy (and you) forwards. It may be easiest at this stage to think of the escaping air as a small motor which pushes the canopy (and you) in the direction that you are facing. This imaginary motor is the inherent forward speed of the canopy and in the case of the 'double L', this inherent canopy speed is about five miles an hour. Also, assuming the average weight of a parachutist to be about 12 stone, or 170 lbs, the canopy's rate of descent is about 18 feet a second; therefore, on an average descent where the canopy is deployed at 2,500 feet, it will take the average parachutist about $2\frac{1}{2}$ minutes to reach the ground. Theoretically, therefore, IN STILL AIR it is possible to move around the sky at 5 m.p.h. in whichever direction you are facing; if you face in exactly the same direction for the $2\frac{1}{2}$ minutes of your descent, you would cover about 365 yards.

Now the whole problem of canopy control arrives when you consider the variable wind speed over the DZ combined with the inherent speed of the canopy (the 'still air' condition being virtually non-existent). To take a simple case, assume the wind speed over the DZ is 5 m.p.h. and the inherent speed of your 'double L' is also 5 m.p.h. If the canopy is turned so that you are facing downwind, you will 'run' with the wind at a combined speed of about 10 m.p.h. (The inherent speed of the canopy being added to the speed of the wind over the DZ.) In this condition you would cover about 730 yards across the ground in the $2\frac{1}{2}$ minutes of your descent from 2,500 feet. Yet again, if your canopy is turned into the wind ('holding' the wind), the inherent 5 m.p.h. speed of your canopy will theoretically cancel out the 5 m.p.h. of the wind over the DZ because the two are in direct opposition to one another and you should descend nearly straight down; (actually this does not happen exactly in practice as the wind is unlikely to be a constant 5 m.p.h. all the way down from 2,500 feet). Already you should realise that even with only 5 m.p.h. of wind over the DZ, you have tremendous latitude in where you land.

This diagram shows you an ideal spot for an early descent with a 'double L' in 8 m.p.h. of wind over the DZ.

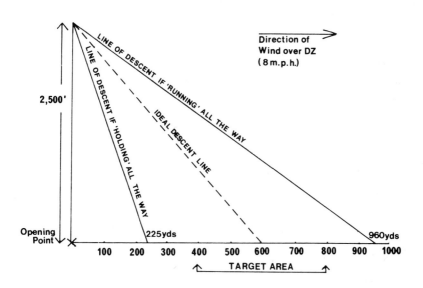

If you 'ran' all the way with the wind you would end up about 960 yards downwind of the point over which you were dropped and if you 'held' all the way into wind you would land only about 225 yards downwind of your opening point. Ideally, therefore, during your early jumps you should be dropped midway between these two extremes to land you in the 'target' area. You will be dispatched over a pre-deter-mined opening point which will allow you to drive part of the way and hold part of the way to land you in the target area. A point worth making at this stage is that for your first twenty or so descents it is only necessary for you to land within the approximate area of the target; so in referring to the target area initially, think of it as any grass area within about a 200 yards radius of the target cross itself.

So that you understand completely how the canopy is controlled you should again look at Figure 9. On the back of the two rear risers you will find the steering toggles, one on each side. Each steering line runs up through a keeper and each is attached to the rigging line which goes up to the outside of each steering window; in the case of the seven-gore spread 'double L' (illustrated) these two rigging lines are numbers 6 and 23. So what happens when the left hand steering toggle is pulled down?

As the left hand steering line is attached to rigging line No. 6, this rigging line is pulled down and this distorts and reduces the effective area of the left hand steering window. The result of this is that relatively more air pressure is permitted to escape through the right hand steering window; therefore the canopy is turned round to the left. Likewise, if the right hand toggle is pulled down, the right hand steering window is reduced in size, relatively more air pressure is forced from the left hand window and the canopy swings around to the right.

Having looked at the theoretical mechanics of canopy control it is logical to follow this with its practical application in the three stages of the descent. Returning to the stage of the magic word 'check', that's exactly what you should do. First grasp the risers and look up so that you can see the entire canopy. Check the canopy for any of the abnor-malities discussed in the last chapter and don't mistake the modification for anything out of the ordinary; it's amazing the number of students who do when they see it for the first time! Follow the check of the canopy by examining the rigging and steering lines down to the risers and steering toggles respectively. All being well, now grasp the steering toggles simply between the second and third fingers of each hand and have a general look around, above and below you. It is unlikely that there will be any other parachutists close to you as plenty of separation should be given between inexperienced jumpers, but this quick look round is a good habit to get into for later on. Having carried out these checks, you should now orientate yourself. The aircraft has run in over the target into wind, and you have exited it facing forwards and over a pre-determined opening point upwind of the target; therefore you can expect to be hanging under the canopy, over this opening point and with your back to the target. If your back is not towards the target it may well be that you have turned around the vertical axis before or during canopy deployment, and in this eventuality it is best to turn so that the target is behind you, otherwise you will find yourself running quite rapidly with the wind while you are checking the opening point. You should now look straight down below to see if you are, in fact, over the opening point. If you are upwind of the opening point ('deep') you can expect to drive a good deal during your descent and, vice versa, if you are downwind of your opening point ('short'), you can expect to hold off for a large part of your descent. If, however, you are to the left or right of your opening point, you are what is termed 'off the wind line'. The wind line is an imaginary line running through the centre of the target in exactly the same direction as the wind; it therefore follows that the opening point is always on the wind line. The wind line is the crux to accurate parachuting, for if you stay too far away from it, it may well be difficult to manoeuvre yourself back on to it before you run out of sky. There *is* an area of manoeuvre away from the wind line which will still permit you an accurate landing and this area is called the 'wind cone', but more of this later. During your first few descents your main problem will be not knowing your exact height above the ground, and how long it is going to take you to descend. Experience is the only way to solve this problem and to this end you should note the size of buildings, vehicles, trees and other familiar objects on the ground during this orientation phase of your descent.

Having orientated yourself, you are now ready to control your parachute towards the target. The easiest way to learn canopy control is to have the DZ Controller or another instructor giving you instructions during your descent. These handling instructions could be given to you verbally with the use of a loud-hailer, or visually, using a signal system similar to the 'bats' that used to be used to land aircraft on aircraft carriers at sea. The first system has the disadvantage that while wearing a closely-fitting helmet you may well find it difficult to hear the necessary instructions, in spite of the use of the loud-hailer. If the second system is employed by your club you can expect to receive a thorough briefing on the signals that you may see. Obviously if either of these systems is used they are of little value unless the DZ Controller (or instructor) gives you a thorough debrief afterwards, explaining exactly why the various instructions were given. All canopy control is exercised by correct use of the steering toggles, and the maxim for all canopies is BE GENTLE. Any violent tugging of the steering toggles will immediately upset the inherent stability and trim of the canopy in flight; additionally, alteration of canopy trim will increase the rate of descent, therefore it is important that from your first descent onwards you get into the habit of pulling down the steering toggles precisely but gently. It's a joy to watch a really good competition parachutist on his approach to the target; you hardly notice any movement of his hands at all, for his sensitive feeling for the canopy is something that has become second nature to him. The turning of the canopy, therefore, is made by pulling down on the toggle on the same side as the direction in which you wish to turn. The faster and further you pull down the toggle, the faster your canopy will turn (and also the higher your rate of descent during this turn). It is best to get into the habit of pulling down the toggles with your hands in front of you so that you can see them. If both steering toggles are pulled down together, the inherent forward speed of the canopy is reduced or 'braked'. You will find that when using a 'double L' canopy, braking is only effective in very light winds, but when you progress to more advanced canopies you will find yourself using the canopy's brakes more and more. Braking is only useful if you are driving with the wind – it is a complete waste of time using the brakes when you are holding off, as the very action of holding off is a means of slowing down your speed across the ground to the target and braking will only reduce its effectiveness.

The ideal approach to the target is made when you actually keep it in sight throughout the descent. Holding off is, therefore, not a very tidy manoeuvre as your back is towards the target and you have to give small turns to left or right to keep a visual check on its relative position. However, I have mentioned holding off as being used for part of the descent from the ideal opening point for two reasons. First, as I have already mentioned, the braking on a 'double L' canopy is not very effective and secondly, during your first few descents you will not readily know just how you can move off the wind line and still be able to get back on it again. This second reason will be a little more clear when you understand the wind cone. Once again, in definition, it is that area of manoeuvre away to either side of the wind line which will still allow you to land on target. Have a look at these two wind cone diagrams (not drawn to any scale).

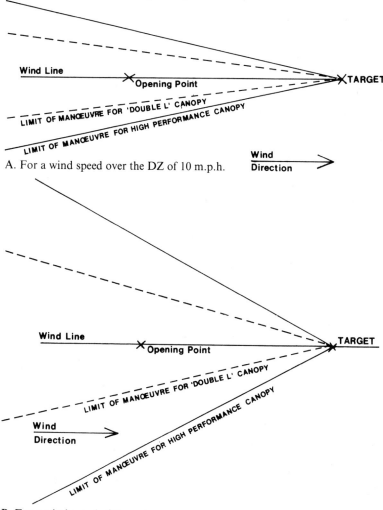

A. For a wind speed over the DZ of 10 m.p.h.

B. For a wind speed of 5 m.p.h.

The purpose of these two diagrams is to show you the comparison of the angles of the wind cone which vary because of two variables, the most usual of which is the wind. The other, which is the inherent performance of your canopy, will only change when you progress to a more advanced type. You should see, therefore, that the less the wind speed over the ground, the more your limit of manoeuvre away from the wind line. Don't expect to see the lines which indicate the limits of the wind cone marked out on the drop zone; they are purely imaginary–I actually heard a student once remark to his instructor after a descent that he hadn't seen the wind cone; he seemed quite surprised!

The three diagrammatic examples given below show the correct path of your canopy for the following three situations:

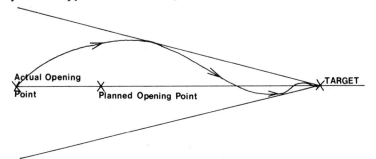

(a) When you find yourself positioned deep (up-wind) of the target on orientation.

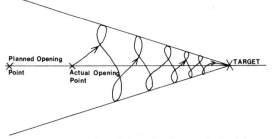

(b) When you find yourself positioned short (or down-wind) of the opening point on orientation.

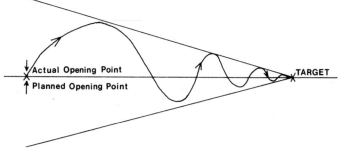

(c) When you find yourself positioned over the opening point itself on orientation

The principle of this practice being that if you are deep you must use the wind to assist you to cover a greater distance across the ground, and if you are short you must reduce the effect of the wind by a concentrated zig-zag path (or by holding off.) The ideal spot will permit you a gentle zig-zag glide path to the target astride the wind line. Of course, you must check your distance from the target at regular intervals during the descent; it may help for you to bear in mind that after about 30 seconds of your descent you should be about a quarter of the way from the opening point to the target, 60 seconds–half of the way, $1\frac{1}{2}$ minutes–three-quarters of the way, and so on. If, during these regular checks of your position you think you are going to overshoot the target (land beyond it), you must obviously rectify this by holding off or by using the concentrated zig-zag pattern. Likewise, if you think you are going to land short of the target, you must make up the extra distance by driving with the wind.

It is only possible in covering the subject of canopy control to give you the basic working principles of guiding yourself to the target area, and essentially practical experience and comprehensively constructive criticism by your instructor are the best ways to perfect these working principles.

The final phase of the descent is the preparation for the landing itself. This phase of the descent, as described now, should be used for at least your first thirty descents and a more advanced form of preparation for landing will be discussed towards the end of this chapter when considering high-performance canopies and 'setting up' for downwind landings. For this early stage of your progression there are two important principles which you must adopt. First, you must have your canopy turned directly into wind for your landing and, secondly, you must avoid any substantial manipulation of the canopy within 250 feet (about 15 seconds) of the ground. The reason for the first requirement is the need to cut down (or, at best, completely eliminate) your horizontal movement across the ground; by turning your canopy directly into wind its inherent forward speed will be in direct opposition to the wind. The reason for the second requirement has already been mentioned; any pulling down of the steering toggles will upset the trim of the canopy and increase its rate of descent–obviously it is best to land with a stable canopy, descending as slowly as possible. So at about 300 feet you should be positioned over the target area and it just remains for you to turn the canopy through 180 degrees to turn directly into wind.

Your instructor should have pointed out a suitable reference on the ground which you should be facing before you land. Also, remember to keep an eye on the windsock in case the direction of the surface wind has altered during your descent. Once you are facing into wind you should adopt the parachute landing position (described in the next chapter) in final preparation for the actual moment of touch-down.

Before going on to the look at the handling of high-performance canopies it is relevant to make the point that the suspended harness is, once again, a valuable training aid. Every stage of the descent will become more familiar to you if practised in the suspended harness, so that when you are hanging in the real harness, much of the initial mystery of canopy handling will have been removed.

Although individual instructors may have differing views on students' progression from simple canopies through to high-performance canopies, the following is the BPA accepted standard:

Up to Category V–Double L

Category V – Category VIII–1.6 7TU

Category VIII and above – Para-Commander or equivalent

The 7-gore TU is shown in Figure 4. Its control system is the same as the Double L, but its inherent forward speed is about 8 m.p.h. (nearly four metres per second) and its rate of descent is about 16 feet per second (or five metres per second.) It is not necessary to go into detail about the control of the 7-gore TU as basically it is a stepping-stone in the progression to the Para-Commander type of canopy. However, it should be pointed out that you should always treat any new canopy (with a more lively performance) with a good deal of humility and respect. This is true with any progression from Double L to 7TU; from 7TU to Para-Commander, and from PC to the new breed of Ram-Air canopies. You must remember that although you may be quite an expert on one particular type, the next step up will mean you become a relative novice again. Although better performance generally means faster forward speed and slower rate of descent, it also means more braking power (which, if overdone, will result in a stall and rapid rate of descent) and more inherent instability. The inherent quality of increased braking power can be a considerable advantage as you will see later, but increased instability is a disadvantage of which you must be aware; any slight movement of the steering toggles will more readily upset the trim of the canopy. Therefore a golden rule might well be: the more advanced a canopy is, the more gentle you must be when controlling it.

The Para-Commander was introduced to sport parachuting by the Pioneer Parachute Company in the summer of 1964, based on a revolutionary design by a Frenchman, Pierre Lemoigne. It was revolutionary because of its inherent 'lift' characteristic caused by the slots shown in Figure 10, the apex being pulled down to produce a greater controllable air pressure within the canopy and its stabilization panels on either side. There are many other canopies of a similar type available: Security's 'Crossbow', GQ's 'Dominator' and 'Pathfinder', the French 'Olympic' and the Czechoslovakian KRAS-PTCH-8, to name but a few; however, the Para-Commander (or PC) is used as the example throughout because of its world-wide popularity.

The manufacturers of the PC claim a forward speed of about 13 m.p.h. (nearly 6 metres per second) and a rate of descent of about 13 feet per second (4 metres per second). This gives us an idea of its performance compared with a 7TU, from which you can see that these characteristics give you the ability to cover much more ground and also more time to control your descent to the target.

If only one toggle is pulled down a short way (to about 8 inches), the four steering slots on that side will only alter slightly, whilst the rear slots and opposite steering slots will still allow a normal escape of air pressure. The result of this is a very lazy, large radius turn which is not really acceptable. Pulling down the toggle even further will induce an unstable oscillation, the violence of which is directly proportional to the speed at which the toggle is pulled down. The simplest way to understand the control of the PC is to bear in mind that the pulling of a steering toggle tends to invert the steering slots and cause loss of lift on that side of the canopy; this causes a banking effect to that side in much the same way as an aircraft.

For normal control of the PC it is preferable to fly it in a permanent condition of half brakes. When both steering toggles are pulled down simultaneously, both sides of the canopy lose lift and cause an increase in the rate of descent and a slowing of forward speed. It may be easiest to think of the stages of braking as the half brakes condition, the full brake condition (where the PC glides with the minimum amount of lift and forward speed) and, finally, the stall condition. In the stall condition the toggles have both been pulled down to an extent which causes more air to escape through the inverted steering slots than is escaping out of the rear slots. The canopy will then stop gliding, shudder and stall with the rear of the canopy descending while the front climbs.

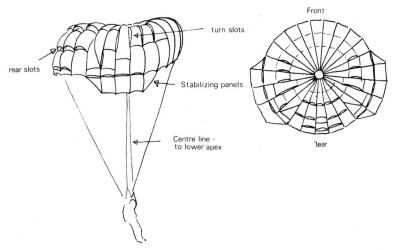

Fig. 10. The 'Para-Commander'. The most popular sport parachute (About 20,000 made since 1964)

When it rocks backwards (with you beneath it having swung forwards) it then begins to sink at a speed which is more than twice its normal rate of descent. The stall condition is thus a useful means of intentionally losing height without holding off or using concentrated zig-zagging. Before you ever adopt the stall condition, you must know how to recover from it. If you were to simply let go of the toggles, the result would be terrific (and, if near the ground, downright dangerous!); the canopy would immediately have its forward speed and lift restored, and during its initial violent acceleration you, (suspended below), would be figuratively 'left behind'; obviously your body has to follow the canopy so then you would swing forward again with terrifying speed. So that is not the way to recover from the stall! The first correct way is normally considered too slow for general use: the toggles are simply allowed to rise up slowly under control. The second and most usual method of stall recovery is known as 'double clutching'. The idea is to keep the canopy stable and directly overhead during the return to the condition of full brakes. Simply raise the toggles smoothly and precisely to shoulder height, pause momentarily and then pull them down to the full brake position. This action restores lift but does not permit a sudden surge forward. The 'double clutch' technique will require a good deal of practice to produce a stable result.

The most stable way to turn the canopy is the turn from the normal flying condition of half brakes. Here you pull down on the toggles on the side to which you wish to turn whilst keeping the other toggle in the position of half brakes. The result is a stable, flat turn. If you wish to turn over a particular point on the ground the stall turn is used. This is initiated from the full brake position with the turn toggle being pulled on down into the stall area. The canopy stops its glide and rotates without covering any distance across the ground. To stop this turn the double clutch described above should be used for the turn toggle.

The position for the conditions of half brakes, full brakes and the stall itself must be discovered by individual experiment, and therefore the initial acclimatisation and mastery of the PC's characteristics will take longer than for a conventional canopy. The spot for the PC should be further upwind than for the TU, in spite of its normally being flown in the half brake condition, and its flexibility lies in its reserve of speed which you can use should the situation demand it; normally to make up extra ground. The control of your PC to the target area is made as already described earlier in this chapter, with two important differences: first, you should fly the canopy on the basis of half brakes throughout the descent, and secondly, you have more room for manoeuvre away from the wind line. The performance of a PC makes it the ideal vehicle for precision landing, and all precision landings are taken downwind. But a word of warning here: do not attempt any downwind landings until you are thoroughly familiar with the handling characteristics of your PC, always turn the canopy into wind for your landings as previously described and avoid any canopy manipulation below 300 feet. Downwind precision landings and the setting up for them will be described in detail in Chapter 15.

It would be wrong to consider that the PC is the last word in parachute canopies; already Ram-Air canopies are becoming more popular, with their lower rates of descent and high forward speeds. Future canopy development remains a matter of speculation but the following points are worth remembering when progressing to a more advanced parachute. First, follow any manufacturers' instructions there may be, secondly obtain all the information you can from other parachutists who have already jumped the canopy and from any articles in parachuting magazines, and finally, when you actually come to jump it yourself, treat the canopy with a good deal of caution and respect.

But whatever the canopy you use, you must eventually touch down, and parachute landings are the subject of the next chapter.

Jerry Irwin

A 'Ram-Air' parachute—in this case a 'Cloud'

Chapter 9

The Landing

It's realistic to point out that most sport parachuting injuries are sustained during the actual landing itself, but it's also reasonable to say that the majority of these injuries could have been avoided had the jumpers concerned adopted the correct techniques. A correct parachuting position on landing will also usually bring you down safely in the event of your landing off the drop zone on hard, uneven surfaces, or in the event of your mishandling the canopy close to the ground. The importance of landing facing into wind has already been stressed and so, having turned the canopy into wind, you must now adopt the parachuting position in final preparation for touch down. Let us examine this parachute landing position in detail. (See Figure 11.)

First, your arms should be up grasping the toggles (or risers), with the elbows tucked in forwards to avoid your taking part of the impact on the point of the elbow itself. Secondly, your head should be bent forward with your chin forced down on to your chest; this negates the possibility of your head whipping back and striking the ground during a backward landing. (This is more commonly called a 'head whip' and is a potentially dangerous occurrence.) Thirdly, you should be watching the ground. This is important so that you can see in what direction you are moving over the ground (it's unlikely that you will be coming *straight* down, particularly during your first few descents). It may be argued that this is not a good teaching and that you should watch the horizon, for if you watch the ground, its apparent last-minute rushing up to meet you may cause you to tense up and resist it. I don't subscribe to this. Plenty of practice will eliminate this tendency, and anyway, you must start watching the ground sooner or later so it might just as well be during your first descent. There is no doubt that for your first few descents the ground *will* suddenly appear to jump up at you during the last 30 feet (or two seconds) and this is something of

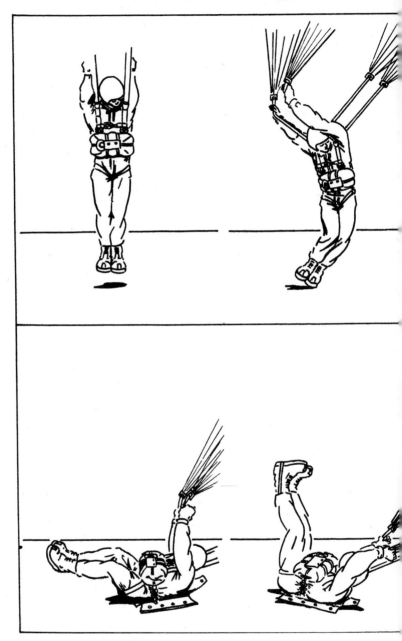

Fig. 11a. Side left landing

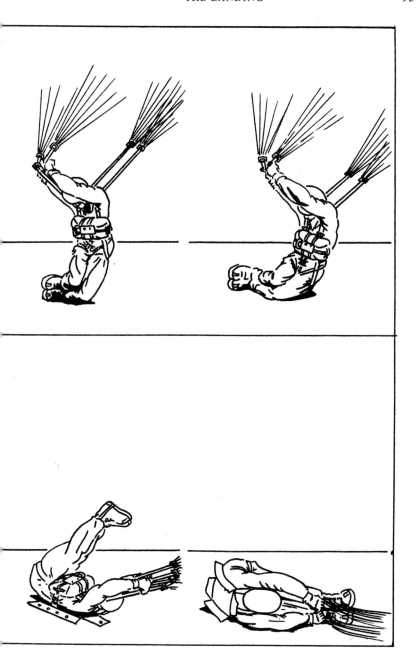

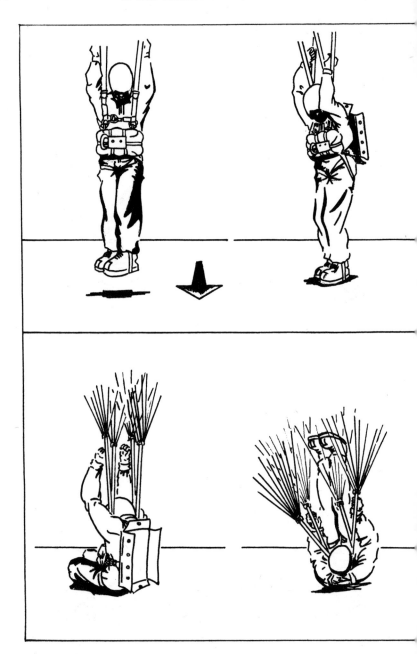

Fig. 11b. Forward left landing

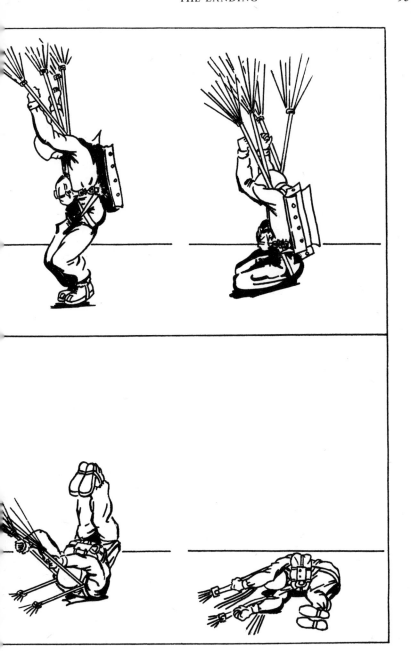

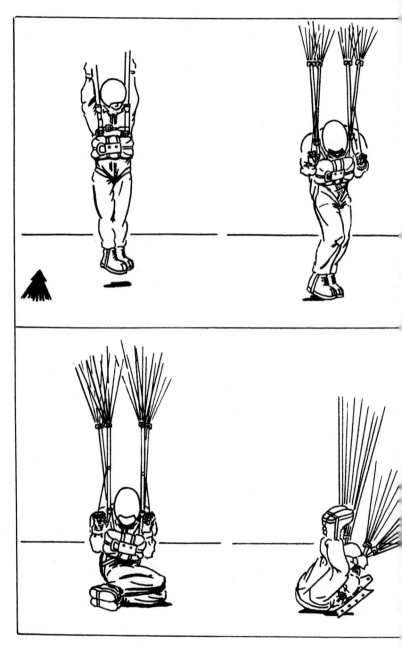

Fig. 11c. Back left landing

which you should be aware. Fourthly, your back should be rounded, your knees slightly bent (so you can just see the toes of your boots over your knee-caps), the soles of your boots parallel to the ground and, most important of all, your feet and knees should be pressed tightly together. The knees are bent so your legs have a natural resilience on touch down which they would not have if they were kept straight. Normally when you jump off a bus or down the stairs a subconscious reflex makes you touch down with your toes first; this should not be allowed to occur during parachute landings as you are not always travelling forwards. You may land in any direction and therefore it is important that your feet are parallel to the ground. And your feet and knees are kept tightly together throughout so that one leg is given physical support by the other during touch down. The final requirement for a good parachute landing position is that the whole body should be sufficiently relaxed for the landing to be made without its offering resistance to the ground, but at the same time, tense enough for you to maintain control throughout.

The parachute landing position is adopted so that the actual touch down is made in accordance with the two principles of a good landing. These principles are first, to absorb the shock of touch down by distributing it evenly over the body and secondly, to permit only those parts of the body which are best suited to absorb the shock of touch down to come into contact with the ground.

These two principles are applied by taking the initial shock of touch down on the feet, with the ankles, knees, hips and back flexing and the shock then being spread progressively along the side of the leg, the thigh and the buttocks, and diagonally across the rounded back to the opposite shoulder. Therefore you can see that the shock is distributed through the body and the vulnerable parts are not allowed to come into contact with the ground.

As you could be travelling in any direction across the ground just before touch down, it is important that you can take a landing in any direction. Landings can be categorised as side landings (left and right), forward landings (left and right) and backward landings (left and right). To understand each type of landing fully, you should study Figure 11. The simplest to master initially are the side landings as just before touch down, your feet are naturally at right angles to your line of drift across the ground. As you approach the ground sideways you should push your legs slightly into the line of drift to assist you in touching down on the soles of your feet together. As the feet touch, the upper part of the body is turned so that the roll finishes on the opposite shoulder. (If you are taking a side right landing, the right shoulder is turned forwards and if a left side, then vice-versa.) For the forward landings, your feet should be turned off to left or right to be as near right angles to the forward line of drift as possible. If your toes are pointing diagonally to the left, then a forward *right* landing will be taken, and vice-versa. The forward landing is then taken as already described, with the upper part of the body turning so that you finish the roll on the opposite shoulder. The backward landing is almost exactly opposite to the forward landing with the exception that your legs should be pushed back slightly from the hips to take the initial shock. Here again, the feet are turned off to be as near right angled to the line of drift as possible, and the landing proceeds as already described.

A good deal of time will be spent on your being taught and practising parachute landings during your initial ground training so that they become completely second nature. Initially your parachute landings will be practised from a standing position (either on grass or matting) so that your instructor can guide you through it slowly, explaining each point of contact as your reach it. You will progress then to jumping from a stationary position on a low bench, and the landing is made slightly more quickly. When you have mastered this stage, you will speed up the landing and jump from a greater height until you can confidently execute a fast forward landing from a four-foot ramp. In fairness to you your instructor should not allow you to jump until you can make a supple, competent landing in any direction, and here again, practice makes perfect. The final point that must be made is that it is imperative you adopt and maintain the described parachute landing position before and during the touch down. The most usual fault is to point your toes and to reach for the ground – you're going to land sooner or later anyway, so remember – arms up; elbows tucked in; head bent forward; chin on chest; back rounded; watch the ground; feet and knees together, the former parallel to the ground and the latter slightly bent; and finally, be semi-relaxed.

Having touched down safely, you must now collapse the canopy. During your early parachuting days you will jump only when the winds are light and therefore it is most unlikely that the canopy will collapse on its own anyway. It is important that you stand up as soon as possible after the descent so that the DZ controller can see that you are unhurt;

if you just lie on the ground (through relief, perhaps!) it's a sure sign for a host of jumpers to come to your assistance.

The first and easiest way to collapse the canopy is to get to your feet as briskly as possible, having made the correct parachute landing roll and then run around the canopy, turning it out of the wind. The second way is known in the United States as the 'Buddy System' – simply because another jumper (or buddy!) grabs the apex or lower peripheral band of the canopy and turns it out of the wind for you; this system is fine if you have a buddy handy! The third way, which you would use if the wind prevented you from jumping up and running around the canopy, is to pull in a handful of rigging lines near the ground and keep pulling them in hand over hand until the canopy collapses. Initially, you should not have to use the final method as you should not be jumping in high enough wind speeds to necessitate it; it is the canopy release method whereby one set of risers is jettisoned by using a Capewell release. It should only be used if all of the previous three methods have been ineffectual and even then the Capewell release should *not* be used after you have touched down.

The final part of this chapter deals with abnormal and emergency landings, the first of these being landings taken on hard surfaces (runways etc.) and high wind landings (the latter being caused by a sudden increase in wind speed during your descent as you should not be jumping outside the limits – remember?). Before a landing under such conditions, the tendency might well be to tense up but it is important that this is not allowed to happen. All you can do is to adopt a really compact parachuting position as already described with the emphasis on keeping your feet and knees tightly together, your elbows tucked in and your chin pressed firmly down on to your chest. You will more than likely find that the landing will be easier than you expected, simply because you will be concentrating more than usual on the correct parachute landing position. A further type of landing is just an extension of the hard surfaces landing, and that is the landing taken into the side of a building. All that has been discussed still applies, but as you are not going to land on your feet initially in this case, you should try and turn either the canopy or your body so the first points of contact are the rounded shoulder and tucked-in elbows. Whatever you do, don't reach out towards the vertical surface with your feet as you will probably land on them anyway, having first hit the building with the side of your body.

The tree landing is not usually as hazardous as it sounds as your rate of descent will be gently slowed as initially you go into and break the thin outer branches before reaching the more solid parts of the tree. Again the position of touch down is important, though slightly different.

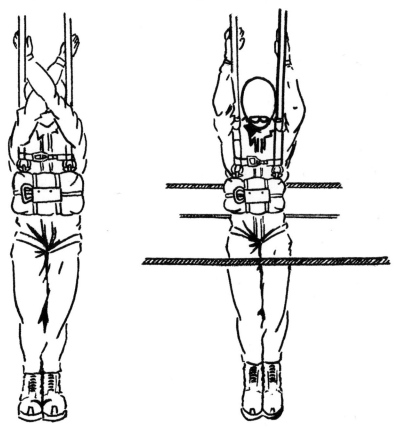

Fig. 12. Tree landing position   Fig. 13. High tension wires landing position

Figure 12 shows the modifications to the normal landing position. Emphasis should be made on keeping your legs tightly together to prevent the somewhat painful possibility of coming down astride a solid branch! Additionally, your elbows should be tucked well forward with your hands on your helmet to protect your face. It is also desirable to close your eyes the second before impact to help protect them from thin branches. You should now maintain this position until your descent is finally stopped; do not try and grab any branches as you pass by. Once you have come to a (dangling?) halt, you can extricate yourself from the harness. The opening of the reserve parachute to provide a type of rope may be necessary if you are suspended too high above the ground to jump down safely. If there is any doubt at all about the safety of your descent from the tree, it is probably simplest to sit tight until your companions arrive suitably equipped with a ladder and/or the local fire brigade!

Landing on high tension cables is potentially the most dangerous type of landing there is. Most parachutists could probably put up with a broken leg, whereas they would be considerably less enthusiastic about getting fried. If a landing on high tension cables is inevitable, it is essential you avoid the eventuality of touching two wires simultaneously; if you just glance off one you might get away with it. The idea, therefore, is to make your body as straight as possible with your arms raised above your head and the palms of your hands placed against the inside of the front risers. (See Figure 13.)

The final abnormal landing is the unintentional water landing (as opposed to the intentional one, which is described in a later chapter). You should never be jumping intentionally within a mile of an open expanse of water unless you are suitably equipped with a life preserver or inflatable Mae West. Therefore, unintentional water landings are only likely in exceptional circumstances, e.g. leaving an aircraft in an emergency over an expanse of water. Once you realise a water landing is inevitable, the following is the drill:

1. Undo the reserve tie-down on one side and unhook the reserve parachute on the same side.
2. Undo the chest strap.
3. Using both hands, force the seat strap forward under your backside so that you are sitting in it.
4. Cross your right hand in front of your face and firmly grasp the left hand risers.
5. Undo both leg straps with your left hand.
6. Grasp the right hand risers firmly with your left hand.
7. Hang on tightly in this position until your feet actually touch the water, then straighten your body sharply and throw your arms straight up above your head. This action will allow you to sink below the harness; you should now swim clear of the main canopy.

Once you are in the water away from your equipment, you are faced with the problem of staying afloat, especially if you are some distance from dry land. First remove your jumpsuit and your boots, the latter which, if they are parachute boots, can be tied together with the laces and hung around your neck to provide temporary buoyancy (up to about 30 minutes before they become waterlogged). Your trousers, with knots tied at the end of the legs and filled with air, can also be used as temporary water-wings, as can your helmet if carefully held to trap air.

Naturally, if you are a non-swimmer and are faced with an unintentional water landing, you will have an additional problem, but do not allow yourself to panic; just apply the above methods of keeping afloat as calmly as you can.

This chapter has dealt with the different types of landing you may encounter and concludes the section on learning to parachute. You have made a substantial start with the sport and now the second section of this book covers your further parachute progression.

Chapter 10

Parachute Packing

This chapter covers the simple maintenance, care and packing of your parachutes. It will not attempt to teach you packing but it will provide a basic guide, as the subject must be personally taught and checks of your progress must be given at particular stages. Once you have been approved competent to pack without supervision, you will be granted a packing certificate by the BPA, initiated by your instructor, which will list the relevant types of parachute. I make no apology for repeating that bad parachute packing is a prime cause of malfunctions and right from the beginning you should develop a state of mind which will not permit you to be slipshod over the care and packing of parachutes. The term 'packing' also covers the inspection of your equipment which, in turn, will lead to your taking care of it and, although the process of packing is straightforward enough, you must never allow yourself to hurry the process to the detriment of your developing skill.

A few general points seem relevant at this stage. When transporting your parachutes it is best to keep them in a bag to avoid chafing, straining, corrosion and other evils which may be caused by unsavoury items in the boot of your car, or wherever. Oil, grease and acid are particular enemies of nylon, and appropriate avoiding action should be taken. Avoid placing heavy objects on top of your equipment, the bending of ripcord pins being one possible consequence. Keep your parachutes away from strong heat; this includes direct sunlight as ultra-violet rays adversely affect nylon–if you want to leave your kit in the sun it's but a simple matter to cover it quickly with your jumpsuit. Finally, keep your equipment as dry as you can–more of this, however, in Chapter 17.

Once you have landed safely, there are two possible ways to carry your kit off the drop zone. The first method should be used if the local airfield authorities require you to move off the field quickly, or if you have only a short distance to walk and intend to re-pack your parachute right away. Simply lay out the parachute in a straight line away from you without removing any of your kit. Hold out your arms in a sleep-walking fashion, then bend down and swinging your body from right to left, 'figure of eight' the parachute over your outstretched arms, first the rigging lines, then the canopy and finally, the sleeve and extractor. When you have returned to the packing area simply lay out the para-chute on the table (or on the ground, as the case may be) by allowing it to fall off your outstretched arms in the reverse order, extractor, sleeve, canopy and rigging lines. You can now remove the rest of your equip-ment. The second method is tidier and can be used when you've plenty of time, a long walk, or you have just made your last jump of the day and do not intend to repack immediately. It is called 'field packing'. Remove all your equipment and lay out the canopy in a straight line by pulling the apex. It is best to remove any tangles at this stage and this problem will be discussed shortly. Now pull the canopy into the sleeve by holding the sleeve retaining line in your right hand and sliding the sleeve over the canopy with your left. (A quicker method here is to have a friend hold on to the retaining line while you slide the sleeve over the canopy with both hands.) Having placed the sleeve (with canopy inside) on the ground, you can now plait the rigging lines; to do this, grab a handful of rigging lines about a foot below the sleeve, make a complete loop around your right wrist by twisting your right hand around through $360°$. Now reach through this loop and pull a further handful of rigging line through the loop to form a second loop. Place your left hand through the second loop and grab a further handful of rigging line a foot lower down, pulling it back through the loop to form a third loop, and so on, until the lines are plaited to the risers. During this plaiting you will have been pulling the pack and harness towards you, so now drop the plaited lines on to the open pack-tray. Undo the pack opening bands and fold the sleeve roughly on top of the rigging lines. Finally, place the extractor 'chute lengthways on top of the sleeve and close the two side flaps of the pack over the whole; to keep it closed, fasten four pack-opening bands on to the eyes sewn on to the opposite flap for this purpose, or on to the exposed ripcord flap, snap fasteners. The parachute is now field packed. A word of warning here: NEVER attempt to close the pack neatly using the ripcord – when field packed, the parachute should remain obviously so, to avoid any possibility of it being mistaken for a parachute ready for jumping. To carry the field-packed parachute off the drop zone, simply sling it normally over both shoulders, fasten the chest strap and snap the reserve on its 'D' rings in the normal way.

You may actually pack the parachute on any relatively smooth surface, e.g. a proper packing table, a packing mat, short *dry* grass or simply a clean floor. There should be means of securing the canopy at the apex: a hook at the end of the packing table, a stake hammered into the grass or even a radiator pipe are some examples. At the other end there should again be a securing point for the 'tensioning device', which is a means of applying tension to the stretched out parachute. The left hand and right pairs of connector links are placed over the two vertical tongues on the tensioning device before tension is applied by tightening the web strap. The other piece of packing kit is called a 'line separator' and its job is simply to keep the two sets of rigging lines apart and tidy during the packing sequence.

The parachute should be laid out on the table, or whatever, with the pack tray uppermost and the harness itself underneath (if the parachutist were still wearing the harness he would be lying face down on the table). As far as the canopy is concerned the 'Master' gore is on top with rigging line No. 1 on its left and rigging line No. 28 on its right (a flat, circular 28-gore parachute is used throughout as an example–the packing of high-performance canopies differs only slightly). This top centre gore usually has the manufacturer's name and canopy serial number stamped upon it.

At this stage it may be necessary to sort out any tangles that may have occurred after landing. Tangles are not unusual and you should not be alarmed at their presence. All that is required is a certain amount of patience and a fair knowledge of the types of tangle and how to restore canopy and lines to their correct configuration. You will inevitably find in early days that your patience will be taxed to the extreme when confronted by a nightmarish spaghetti-like mess, but resist the temptation to finish it all with a sharp knife and take your time! A few different types of tangles are discussed below, together with the usually accepted methods of clearing them. In early days, the undoing of Capewell releases to sort out your tangles may well be discouraged for two reasons: first, it may make untangling more complicated until you are experienced and secondly, continual undoing of the Capewells will gradually loosen them off.

The simple inversion is simply recognised. The 'V' shaped tabs (or 'butterflies') where the rigging lines join the lower peripheral band are the wrong way round, with the flat side on the outside, the rigging line numbers and manufacturer's tab are on the inside and at the apex the rigging lines will be found under the upper peripheral band. The simple inversion is removed by running your hand up inside the canopy, grasping the apex and pulling it down through the entire canopy before re-attaching it to the hook, or whatever, at the end of the table. The partial inversion is a little more irksome and is usually caused by pack and harness having been pulled through one of the blank gores. It is recognised by the fact that some of the 'butterflies' are the wrong way round and some are not. This problem is solved by examining both blank gores and you should readily see which one has had the pack and harness pulled through; simply pull back pack and harness through the blank gore concerned.

The next problem with which you may be faced are the various types of twists. The simple twist occurs when either canopy or pack and harness have been turned around and removal is achieved by picking up pack and harness and turning them in the opposite direction until the lines appear to be straight. The complex twist is when canopy and pack or harness have been pulled through between the two groups of rigging lines; by holding a pair of risers up in each hand, it is a simple matter to turn the pack and harness back between the rigging lines in the opposite direction to the twists until they appear to be clear. Although in both these instances the lines now appear to be clear, there may still be a tangle. The tangle can be very complex and may vary in type, but the following will always apply. First start to solve the problem from the canopy end, never the riser end. Now find the master gore (lines 1 and 28) and loosely holding one in each hand, move gradually down the table towards the risers. When your hands have travelled as far as the tangles permit, you should see how they have developed and be able to pull the pack and harness up underneath the offending group of rigging lines. There may be more than one group of rigging lines causing the obstruction and you must take each group in turn. With the more complex tangles, however, there can be no substitute for experience as all the combinations of tangles can never be written down!

Now it is time for the line check. Holding the left fourteen rigging lines loosely in the right hand, move up towards the canopy. When you reach the lower peripheral band, pull your hands apart until there is one gore's width between them. This will expose the top centre gore (the master gore)–lines 1 and 28 and the bottom centre gore–lines 14 and 15. Now take lines 1 and 14 in the left hand and 15 and 28 in the right and glide your hands down the lines to the connector links. The lines should be clear as follows: line 1 direct to the inside of the top left connector link, line 14 direct to the inside of the bottom left connector link, line 28 direct to the inside of the top right connector link and line 15 direct to the inside of the bottom right connector link. The line check will show you that all the lines are clear and in the correct order if the four principal lines, 1, 14, 15 and 28, are themselves clear.

Once the lines are clear you are ready to pack the parachute. During packing you should get into the habit of inspecting your equipment for faults. When you purchase the equipment, initially a thorough inspection should be made by an instructor or qualified rigger, but after that it is your responsibility to spot any faults and, no matter how minor they may appear, point them out to your instructor right away. The following points give a guide as to what to look for. Starting at the top, the extractor 'chute should be checked for holes, tears and loose stitching. The spring should not be noticeably weak and should be securely attached to the extractor itself. The bridle line should be untwisted, not worn and should be securely tied to the sleeve with a bowline. A bowline should also be used to attach the sleeve retaining line to the sleeve AND to the loop at the bottom end of the bridle line. The top and bottom of the sleeve are likely spots for damage, so check them carefully for tears and loose stitching. The canopy itself should be checked for sears, tears and burns (remember, nylon rubbing against nylon causes burning), especially the top three or four feet from the apex, which is the 'pressure' area–so called because it suffers the greatest stress during canopy deployment. Stains of oil, grease, acid etc. should also be detected and neutralised on advice from your instructor. The rigging lines should be checked for fraying or burning and all hardware should be checked for corrosion, cracking, bending etc. Every once in a while, check that the screws in the connector links are tight. The pack and harness should be checked for chafing, worn stitching, straining and tears; and the pack opening bands checked for strength. Eventually, all these little checks will become second nature but they are, nonetheless, an important part of packing.

Now for the packing itself; first secure the apex and straighten up the upper peripheral band, then apply tension using the tensioning device. Starting with rigging line No. 15, taken from underneath the right hand group of lines with the right hand, pleat each gore in turn (16, 17, 18 . . . 26, 27, 28, 1, 2, 3 . . . 12, 13, 14). To pleat each gore, take the relevant rigging line in succession in the left hand and move it out to the right and back, and place it in your right hand. This action will pleat each gore over to the right of its predecessor in the sequence. When the sequence is complete you should be holding all the rigging lines in your right hand, with lines 1 to 14 between your thumb and forefinger, and lines 15 to 28 between your forefinger and your second finger. With your left hand insert lines 14 to 1 (in that order) into the left hand slot of the line separator, and lines 15 to 28 (in that order) into the left hand slot of the line separator. Now flick the whole set-up over to the left and on to the table, so that the line separator is the correct way up, with lines 14 and 15 at the bottom of the left and right hand slots and thus nearest to the table. All this will be difficult to understand until it has actually been demonstrated to you, but you will be amazed how easily you pick it up. If you're left-handed, perhaps you had better read this backwards, or carry out the actions standing on your head! To continue: each gore should now be pleated neatly in turn, working from the bottom upwards on each side. At the end of this stage you should have fourteen gores pleated out carefully to each side, with their sections of the lower peripheral band neatly aligned; you are now ready for instructor check number one. (See Figure 14.)

After your instructor has carried out the first check, the next action is to fold the lower peripheral band on each side through 90° so that they lie along the centre line of the pleated canopy. Each side is now folded inwards into thirds down the length of the pleated canopy so that the next step may be carried out, which is the sliding of the sleeve over the folded canopy until the mouth of the sleeve is in line with the lower peripheral band. Now gently ease off the tension and remove the connector links from the tensioning device. The next step is the stowing of the rigging lines; to do this, open the protector flap at the bottom of the sleeve to real the rigging line retaining, elastic bands and check that these are unbroken. Having replaced any broken elastic bands, grab all the rigging lines in one hand about two feet below the peripheral band and pull them up towards the top of the sleeve (this action will, of course, pull the pack and harness up also). Lay the lines on the sleeve so that they run from its mouth, up between either set of elastic bands and round and down to the right hand side of it to the pack and harness. Next close the mouth lock over and pull the top two elastic bands

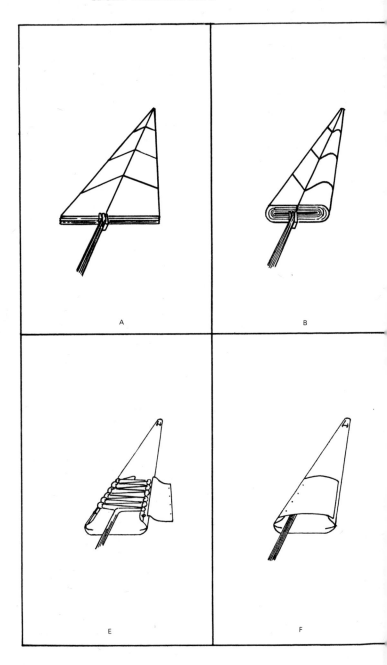

A

B

E

F

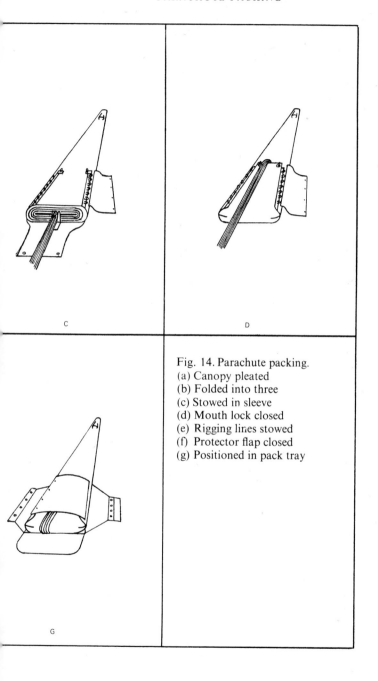

C

D

Fig. 14. Parachute packing.
(a) Canopy pleated
(b) Folded into three
(c) Stowed in sleeve
(d) Mouth lock closed
(e) Rigging lines stowed
(f) Protector flap closed
(g) Positioned in pack tray

G

through the two holes in the mouth lock. The stowing of the lines themselves can now begin, and only practice will allow you to make a neat job of this. By pulling up enough line to make a loop, open each elastic band in turn from top to bottom and stow each successive loop within its respective elastic band until all the rigging lines have been stowed neatly from side to side, with the outside of each loop being positioned almost to the edge of the sleeve. At the completion of this stage there should be three or four inches of rigging line unstowed, the risers should be neatly placed in pairs and the pack tray lying open to receive the sleeved canopy and stowed lines. You are now ready for instructor check number two.

The next step, with which your instructor will probably help you, is to release the apex, stow it within the top of the sleeve and then 'figure of eight' the sleeve retaining line and likewise stow that in the top of the sleeve. The ripcord cable should now be slid through the ripcord housing from the housing from the harness end and the handle itself stowed in the ripcord pocket. Now close the protector flap at the bottom of the sleeve, grasp each side of the bottom of the sleeve with both hands and move the whole sleeved canopy down until the bottom of the sleeve is level with the bottom of the pack. Next, gently lifting each side of the sleeve in turn, check that the risers run neatly down the pack tray without any twists. The next fold is only taken as far as the top of the rigging line protector flap on the sleeve and the reason for this is to make the folds level thereafter. Each successive fold is made level with the top and bottom of the pack respectively. Before actually closing the pack you are ready for your instructor's last check, number three.

The closing of the pack may be achieved in one of two ways. The first is to 'figure of eight' the bridle cord and extractor' chute on to the top of the folded sleeved canopy, and then close the two side flaps, engaging the two centre grommets over the two centre locking cones. The third and fourth pins should then be placed through the second and third cones respectively. The top flap can now be closed and its cone pushed up through the top grommets on the two side flaps. The top (or first) pin should now be pushed through the top cone. Now, pressing down firmly on the centre of the pack, remove the third and fourth pins from the second and third cones and replace them with the second and third pins respectively. The fourth pin is now free to be placed through the bottom cone when this has been pushed up through the bottom grommets on the two side flaps. The whole pack can now be tidied up by tucking away loose flap ends at top and bottom. All that remains is to do up the four pack opening bands on either side. There is no need to close the ripcord protector flap as it would have to be undone for your pre-emplaning 'pin' check. The second method of closing the pack is found by some to be simpler. The top cone (on the top flap) is placed through the top grommet on the two side flaps and the top (or first) pin is placed through it. The extractor 'chute is then compressed as described above and the second pin is pushed through the second cone, which in turn has been pushed up through the second grommet. The third and fourth pins are then pushed home in turn through their respective grommets and the final touches are completed as already described. The use of either of these two methods is purely a matter of personal preference. Finally, all that remains to be done is to sign the packing card for that particular parachute.

Although the above procedures for packing the main parachute apply basically for all main parachutes, some of the new wing and foil canopies DO have a few differences and in these cases, the manufacturer's own particular instructions should be followed very carefully. The procedures for packing the reserve parachute are very similar, but will not be explained in the same amount of detail. It is essential that the reserve parachute is repacked at not more than three-monthly intervals and the repacking date recorded and signed on the packing card.

First, lay out the canopy, sort out any tangles and apply tension as already described. Next, carry out a line check (remember, the lines are 1 and 24, 12 and 13 for a 24-foot flat circular reserve). The same inspection procedures as relevant should be applied when packing the reserve. Now pleat the canopy, place the rigging lines in the line separator and count out the twelve gores tidily to each side as with the main. After instructor check number one you have the essential difference between main and reserve. As there is no sleeve on the reserve (to speed deployment . . . remember?) the rigging lines are stowed *before* the canopy. After tension is released, stow the rigging lines in the elastic bands located in the reserve pack tray itself, starting from the pack tray end of the lines. After instructor check number two, the canopy is folded into three, the apex released and the pack tray opened out and turned through 90° to receive the canopy. The canopy is then lifted and folded on to the pack tray in much the same way as the sleeved main. After instructor check number three the pack may be closed, and your instructor will undoubtedly help you do this as it can be quite a struggle. The top and bottom flaps should be closed first and the pins of another ripcord handle used to temporarily prevent these two flaps opening while the end flaps are then themselves closed; the proper ripcord is then finally placed in position. *Never* use horrors called temporary packing pins. These are individual pins whose 'temporary' presence can be easily overlooked so if you find any in your club, throw them as far as you can; it's much safer and just as simple to use another ripcord. Finally, tidy up the reserve by tucking in any loose part of the flaps and hook up the pack opening bands.

The rigging of the static line for student parachuting has been deliberately excluded from the preceding paragraphs as the entire static line procedure is covered at length in the final chapter.

Finally, remember that a safe parachutist is a careful parachutist and this is often reflected in the way he packs his parachute. Take a pride in your packing and be meticulous over the maintenance of all your equipment.

Chapter 11

Free Fall and the Category System

This chapter covers your student progress by explaining the category system. The British Parachute Association classification system of categories of sport parachutists provides us with a minimum standard of progression which may be achieved by an above average student. The words 'minimum' and 'above average' are important for it should be realised that very few students will actually achieve this rate of progression. You will be carefully guided through this systematic progression by your instructor and although your natural enthusiasm may make you press him for a faster progression, you must remember that his basic concern will be for your own safety.

Category I

Has been passed out on Basic Ground Training (six hours minimum) and is ready for first static line descent.

This is straightforward enough. I have outlined your basic ground training programme for you in Chapter 4 and once your instructor is satisfied that you are sufficiently trained (and this may take considerably longer than the permitted minimum of six hours) he will classify you as a Category I parachutist.

Category II (from 2,500 ft. AGL)

(a) Has performed a *minimum of three absolutely stable observed static line descents in the full spread position* (counting throughout).

(b) Has completed a total of thirteen hours of ground training in accordance with the BPA Minimum Ground Training Programme.

Again this is self-explanatory. You must perform three absolutely perfect static line descents in the full spread position before being allowed to progress to dummy ripcord pulls. Once again Chapter 4 provides you with the outline of the thirteen hours of ground training.

Category III (from 2,500 ft. AGL)

Has performed a *minimum of three successful and consecutive observed static line descents with dummy ripcord* (counting throughout).

We now come on to something new. Before your instructor will permit you to progress to free fall you must be classified as a Category III parachutist by performing three consecutive and perfect dummy ripcord pulls. The descent is similar to those you have already achieved as a Category II parachutist with the essential difference that you are actually going through the motions of pulling the ripcord, the main parachute still being static line operated. Before you emplane a dummy ripcord handle will be placed in the pocket on the harness and ideally you will have had a practice session in a stabilised harness (one that suspends you in a stable face-to-earth position) to perfect the drills. The count is the same as for Category II but the actions are different:

One thousand... force yourself hard into the basic spread position on exit from the aircraft. It is essential you hit this position instantly.

Two thousand... glance down at the handle (without bending your head forward) and simultaneously bring both hands into the position of the pull with the right hand grasping the dummy handle. (Left hand above the head, right hand on handle.)

Three thousand... thrust out arms to the original stable position with the dummy handle still grasped in the right hand.

Four thousand... *check*... exactly the same as before but after the check place the dummy handle over the right wrist for safe retention before reaching up and grasping the toggles.

The dummy ripcord pull is a little unrealistic as the canopy deployment sequence is well under way before you have actually pulled the dummy handle; but you must avoid the tendency to hurry the pull and have the handle out before canopy deployment. The secret to the good dummy ripcord pull is twofold: first hit a really good stable position at 'one thousand' and secondly, ensure a good recovery to the stable position on 'three thousand'. The dummy ripcord pull is not easy and you will only achieve three consecutive good ones by plenty of practice on the ground and by concentrating on the exact drills just before exit.

Category IV (5 seconds–from 2,800 ft. AGL)

(*a*) Has performed a *minimum of five stable five-second delayed openings*.

(*b*) Has remained stable throughout opening on each descent.

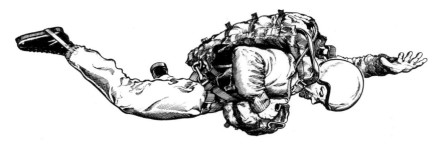

1. Look and reach for ripcord handle.

2. "Pull" and recover.

PULLING THE RIPCORD

Fig. 15. Pulling the ripcord

(*c*) Has looked at ripcord handle before and during the 'reach and pull'.

(*d*) Has achieved reasonable canopy handling.

You will probably find that your first five-second delay is much more memorable than your first static line descent, basically because you are now on your own. Having been passed out as Category III it's back to the 'stabilised harness' again to practise the count and actions for the five-second delay, which are:

Go! . . . One thousand . . . hit the stable position as before, *two thousand . . . three thousand . . .*

Four thousand . . . glance down at the handle (without bending your head forward) and simultaneously bring both hands into the position of the pull with the right hand grasping the handle, left hand above your head,

Five thousand . . . thrust out your arms, recovering to the original stable position with the handle being pulled out firmly by the right hand,

Six thousand . . . seven thousand . . . eight thousand . . . check. Retain the recovered stable position until the check then, all being well, place the ripcord handle over your wrist as already described.

The common tendency is to hurry the count and in some cases to forget all that has been learnt about the stable position from the static line phase of the progression. Don't let these possibilities happen with you; just concentrate on what you are going to do before exit and after exit let your instructor see a good position and let him hear a strong determined count. If, at any stage of the delay you feel yourself becoming unstable or out of control–don't wait–PULL THE MAIN HANDLE IMMEDIATELY.

The final requirement of Category IV is to have 'achieved reasonable canopy handling' and by this stage you will have carried out at least eleven descents which will have easily brought you up to this simple standard.

Category V (10 seconds–from 3,200 ft. AGL)

(*a*) Has performed a minimum of five stable ten-second delayed openings (counting throughout).

(*b*) Has learnt to maintain heading during exit and in free fall.

Once again, the stabilised harness should be used before progression to ten-second delays. The important thing to remember is that by the time you have fallen for ten seconds, you will have accelerated to near terminal velocity (which is reached after about twelve seconds of free fall) because the faster you fall, the more sudden will be the effect of small movements of your limbs on your basic stability.

The actions are the same for Category IV but the count is obviously longer. You will now exit the aircraft at 3,200 feet above ground level.

GO!... One thousand... hit the stable position *... two thousand...* etc ... to *eight thousand ...*

Nine thousand ... look for and grasp the handle, having adopted the position of the pull ...

Ten thousand ... the pull and the recover to the stable position ...

Eleven thousand... twelve thousand... thirteen thousand... check.

Requirement 'b' (the maintenance of your heading) is something that again should be learnt in the stabilised harness and at this stage it is necessary for you to be able to understand and apply basic body turns. By maintaining heading it is simply meant that you remain facing the same direction throughout the free fall phase of the descent; this is normally the same direction in which the aircraft is flying. Having stabilised after your exit you should glance down at the ground and make sure you are not turning, either to right or left. If you find at any time that during your free fall you are moving off heading, you should return on to your original heading by very gently bending your body at the waist, to the left if you are turning to the right, and to the right if you are turning to the left. Once you are back on heading, you should straighten into your original stable position. But as before if you have any tendency towards loss of control or a turn which you cannot stop right away, you must operate the main ripcord handle immediately, at no matter what height you are.

Category VI (15 seconds–from 4,000 ft. AGL)

(*a*) Has performed a *minimum of five stable fifteen-second delayed openings* in the following sequence:
   (1) Two flat stable (counting throughout)
   (2) After instruction in the use of instruments, three flat stable descents using instruments, but countinuing to count throughout.

(*b*) After successful completion of (*a*) has demonstrated ability to perform 360° turns in each direction, stopping on aircraft heading.

This is an important step in your training for after a free fall of 15 seconds your body has attained terminal velocity, about 120 m.p.h.

(or 176 feet per second). Therefore you will find that any movement of your limbs will more readily upset or alter your basic stability–in fact, having reached terminal velocity, you will have gained a more positive control in free fall. Requirement (*a*)(1) is just designed, therefore, to take you to terminal velocity without any additional manoeuvres. The jump will be made from 4,000 feet above ground level. The pull is initiated on *fourteen thousand* . . . activated on *fifteen thousand* . . . and carried through to the *check* after *eighteen thousand*. Requirement (*a*)(2) introduces the use of the altimeter in addition to the normal verbal count. On the climb to altitude in the aircraft you will notice the needle of the altimeter (the latter normally being mounted on the top of your reserve parachute) moving steadily round the dial until it records the jump altitude of 4,000 feet (having been set at zero on the ground). To read the altimeter in free fall is simply a matter of glancing down at it at frequent intervals; do not bend the head right forward and resist any tendency to relax your stable position. You should initiate the pull when the altimeter reads 2,300 feet, which should coincide with your count of fourteen thousand. If your count reaches fourteen thousand before the altimeter reads 2,300 feet, then pull; you may have rushed your count but this isn't the time to work it out! Likewise, if the altimeter unwinds to 2,300 feet before your count of fourteen thousand you should pull immediately for the same reason. At this stage you should also be getting used to how various features on the ground appear from 2,000 feet. Remember, an altimeter is mechanical and, therefore, although it can be relied upon almost all the time, it could just possibly fail and the use of your eyes (or 'eyeballing it' as they say to the west of the Atlantic Ocean) may be a last resort.

Requirement '*b*' calls for accurately carrying out 360° turns (around a vertical axis) in each direction. You will only be required to perform one complete 360° turn during any one jump. Once more to the stabilised harness, where your instructor will show you how to execute gentle and precise body turns. The turn should be started after picking up a reference point on the ground as your heading; now gently bend your body at the waist in the direction you wish to turn (at the same time maintaining the arched back of the stable position). You will find yourself start to turn around the vertical axis and when you find yourself coming around to your reference point on the ground, straighten at the waist and the turn will stop. You may have to turn a little in the opposite direction to stop precisely on heading particularly if you

have built up a little speed. Once again, if you can't stop the turn–
PULL IMMEDIATELY. If your club's stabilised harness has the
ability to swing around a vertical axis, you will get a good deal of
value out of its use before your first proper free fall turn. (See Figure 14.)

Fig. 16. Simple body turn to left

Category VII (20 seconds–from 5,000 ft. AGL)

(*a*) Has performed a *minimum of five stable twenty-second delayed
openings.*

(*b*) Has demonstrated his ability to recover from an unstable
position leaving the aircraft.

(*c*) Has been introduced to spotting.

Requirement (*a*) is self-explanatory. However, during these twenty-
seconds delayed openings, you should once again check your verbal
count against your altimeter (an altimeter and/or stop-watch MUST
be worn on all delays of 15 seconds and longer). In this case, the pull is
initiated on nineteen thousand and carried on through to the 'check'
after twenty-three thousand.

Requirement (*b*) of recovering from an unstable exit is another step
that can first be practised in the stabilised harness. After a dive exit or
forward roll out of the door, it is simply a matter of moving your limbs

sharply into the basic spread position. You will be amazed and exhilarated as your position changes almost instantaneously from an uncontrolled tumble to the basic face-to-earth stable position, to which, by now, you are well accustomed.

The introduction to spotting is the third requirement in this Category, and the art of spotting is dealt with at some length in Chapter 13.

Category VIII (30 seconds–from 7,000 ft. AGL)

(*a*) Has landed within 50 yards of centre of target on a *minimum of three thirty-second delayed opening descents.*

(*b*) Has learnt to track.

(*c*) Has been cleared for self spotting up to 7,000 feet.

With Category VIII there becomes no need for a verbal count during the free fall phase of the descent but a mental count as you pull is still important; even though by this stage you will have become aware of how long the deployment takes.

Requirement (*a*) is not very difficult and providing you have left the aircraft with a good spot (either yours or your instructor's) you should be landing within 50 yards of the target cross all the time anyway.

Requirement (*b*), learning to track, is something new. Tracking is the ability to cover ground horizontally during the free fall phase of the descent and basically it is achieved by forming the body into a crude aerofoil section. Tracking is dealt with in some detail in the next chapter. To ensure that you have mastered the technique of tracking you can expect your instructor to dispatch you from the aircraft about 200 yards off the wind line from the opening point from 7,000 feet; you must then make up this distance in free fall to be judged proficient in this requirement.

Requirement (*c*) is simply an extension of your experience of spotting already started in Category VII.

Up to this stage all details of your performance will have been written up in the remarks column of your log book by your instructor, and it's at this stage that he may well recommend you for 'C' Certificate. The 'C' Certificate entitles you to parachute away from the direct supervision of a BPA Instructor and your instructor is therefore going to ensure that you are competent and safe before recommending you. Holding 'C' Certificate will also entitle you to be a jumpmaster of Category VI parachutists and above.

To obtain your 'C' Certificate just send your instructor's written recommendation to the BPA as explained on page 19.

Category IX

(a) Has demonstrated to an instructor in free fall that he is fully in control of his movements, is aware of other parachutists around him and is capable of taking avoiding action.

(*b*) Has demonstrated his ability to perform aerial manoeuvres, e.g. loops and barrel rolls.

(*c*) Has been introduced to relative parachuting.

The first of these three requirements is straightforward enough, but the last phrase is so important that a special word is necessary. Taking avoiding action of other parachutists is important both in free fall and when hanging under the inflated canopy; but the most critical moments are during canopy deployment. Remember that the lower man always has right of way and if you're in free fall immediately above him as he pulls the ripcord handle you could well be in trouble. The prime rule here is not to be positioned immediately over another parachutist in free fall below about 4,000 feet (people have been known to pull high!) To move away, turn quickly to right or left and track off a few yards, keeping your eye on his pulling hand – if he pulls and you're still over him, you must pull...and fast! In spite of all this being common sense, it is amazing how many collisions do occur because parachutists are not always aware of others around them ALL THE TIME.

The other two requirements are dealt with in detail in Chapters 12 and 14 respectively.

Category X

(*a*) Has been cleared for relative parachuting.

(*b*) Has been cleared for self-spotted descents up to 12,000 feet.

Both these requirements are self-explanatory and are extensions of requirements in earlier chapters. Details of qualifying descents for progression through Categories IX and X should be entered in your log book by your instructor.

Having achieved Category X classification it could be natural to assume that you 'know it all'. Passing your driving test is a useful analogy for, having done so, you learn more about driving every time you take out your car. So it is with parachuting. You learn all the time and the progression from Category X is the gaining of further experience and expertise.

This photograph shows vividly what the sport of parachuting is all about, smiling Ken Vos relaxing at 10,000 ft over Thruxton

Lou Johnson

John and Sally Williams showing it's a married couple's sport

Chapter 12

Simple Aerial Manoeuvres

After you have been sport parachuting for some time, one of your acquaintances will inevitably pose the question, 'What's with this free fall bit?' or words to that effect, and in your attempt to be both non-chalant and awe-inspiring, you may well reply, 'In free fall, a para-chutist can do anything an aeroplane can do–except go up'. In point of fact you won't be very far from the truth and in discussing aerial manoeuvres, there will be times when a direct comparison is not only of interest, but of considerable value.

Most of the manoeuvres can be practised during your progression from Category VIII to Category X, and many of them are mandatory requirements anyway. There is one basic requirement before attempting any of these manoeuvres, and that is your ability to be completely relaxed in free fall; I don't mean 'mind in neutral', but the ability to feel completely at ease and confident of your being able to return to the basic stable position should you momentarily lose control. Before you attempt any new manoeuvres, you will find it most valuable to practice the particular movements of your limbs in the stabilised harness. Once you're sitting in the aircraft on the way up, concentrate on what you are going to do so that when you are actually in free fall, you do not have to waste time thinking about it.

All aerial manoeuvres are initiated and achieved by the movement of some or all of your limbs which either vary the effective surface area of your body, shift your centre of gravity or cause deflection of the flow of air past your body. You will see how these basic principles cause the various manoeuvres as we deal with them.

By now the basic full spread stable position will be second nature to you and, because the position is uncomfortable to hold for long delays, a more relaxed position is called for.

The Frog Position

The frog position is basically a relaxed spread position and once you have grown accustomed to its application, you will seldom use the full spread position. The arching of the back is less strained than the basic position and it is not necessary to force the head back to the same extent. The upper arms should be at 90° to the body, with the forearms bent at the elbows so that the hands are roughly in line with the head. The legs are apart, but not quite as much as with the full spread position, level and bent gently at the knees. As the surface area of this position is less than the full spread position, the rate of descent is increased. To practise the frog position, you should start the descent using your your normal basic position and then gradually relax into it by bending both your arms at the elbows and your legs at the knees. As in the basic position, any lack of symmetry will induce a turn or, worse, instability, so it is essential that you feel your way into the frog position at your first attempt. (see Figure 17)

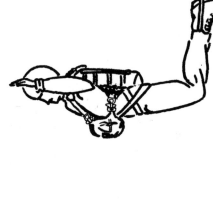

Fig. 17. The frog position

Later you may well find the need for an even tighter position (for 'relative work' or 'style'–see Chapters 14 and 15 respectively) and such a position is called a radical frog. It is simply attained by tightening up the frog position described above: relax the arch even more, pull the arms and hands in much closer to the body and bend the lower legs at the knees even further up towards your head. The alternative position of the legs is favoured by many style jumpers and that is to draw the knees towards the stomach–in reducing your bodily surface area it is even more radical. In this tight position your rate of descent is further increased and control becomes more critical, being exercised by hand movements from the wrist. To slow down your vertical speed, simply push out your arms and legs to the original basic spread position.

The Back-to-Earth Stable Position

Sooner or later during manoeuvres described in this chapter you will find yourself losing visual contact with the earth, and the first time this occurs it might, unless you are prepared for it, cause you disturbing disorientation. The practice of the back-to-earth stable position is good preparation for this insecure, disorientated feeling and it will give you additional confidence. After exit (you *must* be first out of the aircraft from at least 5,000 feet), relax into the back-to-earth stable postion, which is simply the exact opposite of the basic face-to-earth stable position. Your back should be rounded, head pushed forward, arms relaxed with palms facing upwards, with your legs straight and apart. Try and hold the position for a count of ten, in spite of the insecure feeling you will undoubtedly experience. Do *not* trust a chest-mounted altimeter in this position as it is located in a partial vacuum and will not read accurately. To return to the basic face-to-earth stable position simply force your head and arms back, arch your back and you will flip over to see the earth spread reassuringly below you. (See Figure 18.)

Fig. 18. The radical back to earth position

Turns

The simple body turn has already been described in Chapter 11 and methods of speeding up the turn will now be dealt with. Taking the simple body turn as a basis, its speed can be increased by bending back the leg at the knee on the side to which you are turning. A turn from the frog position will automatically be faster because of the increased rate of descent, and here the body and leg turns can be applied in the same way. Additionally from the frog position, your hands can be tilted from the wrist in the direction of turn for increasing the speed still further. The final turn accelerator is the 'push' turn. Here, to speed the right turn you push your right arm downwards towards the earth, and vice versa for a left turn. Thus applying all the principles learnt to date, a really fast right turn could be executed as follows: exit the aircraft, pick up a reference point on the ground, reduce your body to a radical frog position as you gradually build up to terminal velocity. After falling for at least twelve seconds, give yourself a mental command of 'GO!' and simultaneously initiate the turn by pushing hard down with your right hand, tilting both hands to the right from the wrist, bending the body from the waist to the right and by bending back your right lower leg at the knee. The turn will probably surprise you with its speed and you may well rotate twice through 360° before you can stop it! In fact the art of executing a really fast turn is being able to stop it on heading, and this is achieved by initiating a turn in the opposite direction at least 90° before it. Only practice will enable you to execute fast precision turns which can be stopped on a given heading. (See Figure 19.)

The Delta Position

The delta position provides the parachutist with a limited means of making ground horizontally. From the basic stable or frog positions, the legs are straightened about 30° apart and the straight arms (with palms facing downwards) are swept back at anything between 30° and 45° to the body, depending on the required effectiveness of the position. The effect of sweeping back the arms is to lower the head (the effective surface of the upper part of the body being reduced), and the airflow tends to be directed along the underside of the body towards the feet to give a certain amount of forward displacement with the rate of descent increasing at the same time. The more swept back the arms, the more head down the position, and thus the rate of descent increases. The most effective horizontal displacement is achieved with the arms swept back at about 30° from the body; if they are swept back any further,

Fig. 19. Push turn and wrist turn
(*left*) speed up the simple body turn by   (*right*) body and leg turn from the frog
bending the leg.   position

the increase in vertical rate of descent and radical head down position obliterate any horizontal displacement. To turn in the delta position, just move your head and the upper part of your body in the direction in which you wish to turn. The delta position, as you will discover in later chapters, has a number of uses but one is particularly worthy of mention at this stage; that is the recovery from the flat spin. In early days you were taught that if you could not stop a turn or spin, having briefly tried to counter it, you should pull right away, and this teaching should always be applied below 4,000 feet anyway. However, if you have plenty of experience and height, you can use the delta position to recover from the spin. When flying an aeroplane the recovery from an incipient spin is effected by pushing the stick forward and diving out of it; so it is in free fall. If you find yourself unable to counter the spin, simply sweep back your arms into the delta position and you will find yourself out of it. Once out of the spin you can relax into the normal stable position. One final point: never open in a delta position; you are simply travelling too fast. Always slow down from the delta position to the basic spread by at least 500 feet before you pull. This point applies even more to the next manoeuvre, as you will see. (See Figure 20.)

Tracking

Tracking is the ultimate means the parachutist has at his disposal to cover distance horizontally whilst in free fall. The tracking position may be likened to a crude aerofoil section and this is the basis of its success in application. The aerofoil is designed to give lift when it moves forward through the air and in the tracking position your body is achieving maximum lift. If you achieve a really good tracking position it should be possible for you to move across the sky at about 35° from the vertical. Do not expect to master the art of tracking at the first attempt because there is a slight knack to it which is achieved through practice. On exit from the aircraft, face the direction in which you wish to move, then assume a full delta position. From the full delta position, move gradually into the tracking position by pulling in the stomach, pushing up your behind, round your shoulders, straightening the legs a few inches apart, pointing your toes and straightening your arms along your side with the palms facing downwards; your head should be forced back against the top of the back pack. The amount of reverse arch you apply is the key to the secret of mastering the tracking position, and to be successful you must feel your way into position slowly until you experience the exhilaration of building up lift and speed and actually begin to move horizontally. The track may be finely balanced by small movements of the hands and forearms. It is most frequently used when a parachutist discovers he has left the aircraft over the wrong point on the ground and then uses the track to make up the lost distance. Its most important application, however, is to put distance between parachutists before opening, and this will be further explained in Chapter 14. The slowing down from the track is achieved by flaring out to the stable position and here again, don't ever deploy the parachute whilst still in a track; the consequence could cause considerable damage to both you and your parachute canopy as you may well be travelling at about 180 m.p.h.! So make sure you have flared out at least 500 feet before you pull. (See Figure 21.)

The Back Loop

The execution of a back loop is not too difficult but the execution of a really fast, precise back loop requires a good deal of practice. The back

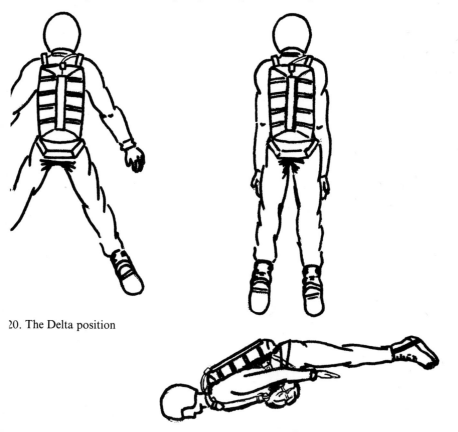

20. The Delta position

Fig. 21. Tracking

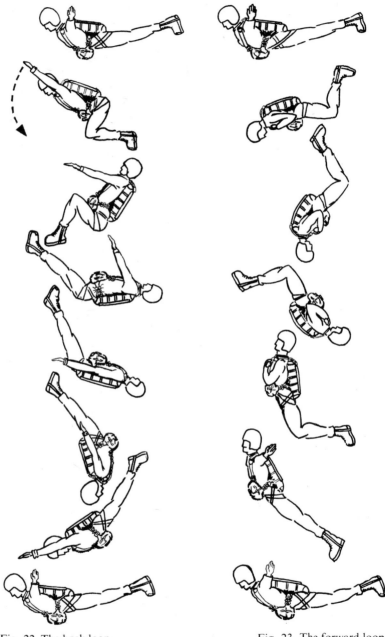

Fig. 22. The back loop   Fig. 23. The forward loop

loop is initiated from any of the stable positions and is achieved by simultaneously pushing violently forwards and downwards with the arms, pulling the knees up sharply to the chest and forcing back the head. The upper part of the body is forced upwards by the airflow and if the loop is started vigorously enough, the momentum will carry you right over. As the earth comes into view again, simply flare out to your original stable position. If the manoeuvre is sloppily performed, you you may well roll off the top of the loop without actually completing it, or come out of it off your original heading. Here again, a mental command of 'GO!' may assist you in starting the loop with enough force, and you may find that keeping your legs and arms slightly apart will help you to remain on heading. (See Figure 22.)

The Forward Loop

The forward loop is not so straightforward. Starting from the stable position extend your legs (keeping them apart for stability), tuck your chin on to your chest and bring your arms right in alongside your chest. Immediately bend forward at the waist, thrusting your head downwards; this will start the forward rotation. As you go over the top, tuck in your your legs and push your hands out to the side. And finally, as the earth comes into view, flare out to your original stable position. (See Figure 23.)

The Barrel Roll

I will describe the movements for the barrel roll to the right; the barrel roll to the left is exactly the opposite. From the stable position, straighten the legs a few inches apart and fold in the right arm across the chest. This will have the effect of turning you over to the right on to your back, and to finish the roll smoothly, simply fold in your left arm over your chest and extend your right. You can assist the movement by twisting your body in the direction of the roll. When the earth comes into view, return to the stable position. If the movement of the arms is unsure and the roll will be also. Practice will ultimately produce a smooth barrel roll on heading. (See Figure 24.)

As no two parachutists are exactly the same shape, size or weight, the manoeuvres described in the chapter will require slight individual variation of technique to perform them successfully. The discovery of these variations can only come about by practice on the ground in a stabilised harness and in the air, and by accurate critique from your instructor. Ultimately you will find great satisfaction in performing a number of different manoeuvres with precision during the same descent; this should be your aim.

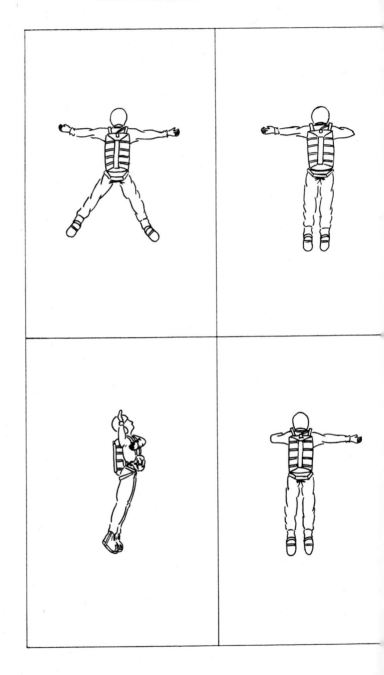

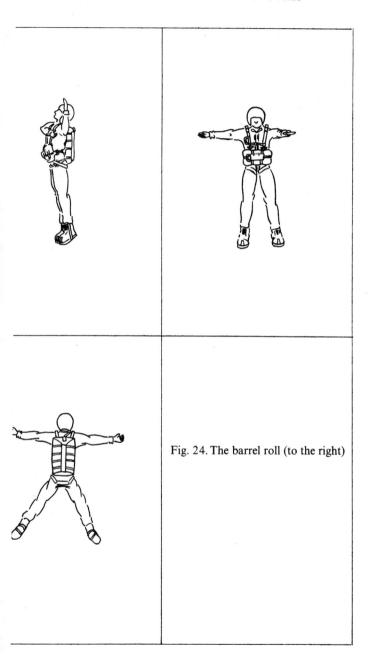

Fig. 24. The barrel roll (to the right)

Chapter 13

Spotting

Spotting is the art of deciding the correct point on the ground over which to leave the aircraft in order to land in the target area and the ability to put this decision to good effect in practise. Spotting is largely dependent on the wind and its varying moods which may very occasionally upset the careful calculations you have made. A good deal of rubbish is always forthcoming, both written and verbal, about how luck plays a large part in spotting; but this is simply an excuse made by parachutists who either treat it too haphazardly or who believe that with sophisticated canopies an accurate spot is simply not necessary. To understand the techniques involved it is easiest to divide the descent into three phases which are, in order of leaving the aircraft, the 'throw forward', the 'free fall drift' and the 'descent under the deployed canopy'. At the moment of exit you are travelling at the same speed as the aircraft and therefore for the first few seconds of your descent you are, in fact, projected forward by the speed of the aircraft. This is the throw forward and its distance is dependent on the speed of the aircraft, the wind speed and direction at exit height and the length of the delay if less than twelve seconds. The free fall drift is that distance you are moved across the ground by the upper winds before canopy development and the descent under the canopy has already been discussed in Chapter 8. (see Figure 25)

To spot an aircraft accurately you should be able to determine the position of two points, the 'exit point', which is the point on the ground over which you actually exit the aircraft, and the opening point, that point on the ground over which you actually open your parachute. As already mentioned in Chapter 8 the determination of the opening point is by use of the wind drift indicator (or streamer). In case you've forgotten, the wind drift indicator is made of a twenty-foot length of crepe paper, ten inches wide with a rod weight taped to one end to

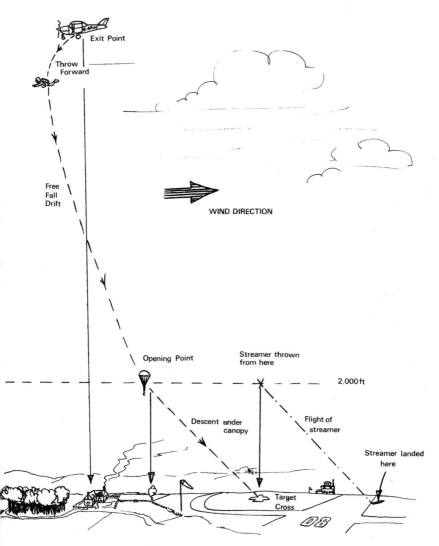

Fig. 25. Spotting (side view)

produce a total weight of between 3 and $3\frac{1}{2}$ ounces. The colour of the WDI is purely a matter of personal preference but obviously light, bright colours are most easily discernible; I find that a WDI half of bright orange and half of bright yellow can be seen very easily against almost all backgrounds. Always have at least two WDIs in the aircraft as it has been known for them not to unroll or even become draped around the tail of the aircraft.

Before taking off the pilot should be briefed to fly directly over the target cross into wind at 2,000 feet above ground level for the streamer run. This briefing is best done using the air photograph of the drop zone which every club should have in its possession. If your club hasn't got one it's but a simple matter to take one yourself the next time a high lift goes up: say to 9,000 feet. The print (at least $10'' \times 10''$) should be mounted on board and have the target cross, the cardinal points of the compass and circles of 200 metres intervals from the target cross marked upon it. If you go to your local flying club you will probably be able to obtain a fablonised compass rose which can simply be stuck to the air-photo (ensuring, of course, that North on the rose, lines up with North on the airphoto). The airphoto should be in the aircraft for the streamer lift and thereafter on the ground so that successive lifts can readily see the run in, exit and opening points. With practice the pilot will be able to judge his climb so that he arrives at 2,000 feet as he passes over the the cross and in this context it is worth mentioning that anywhere between 1,800 feet and 2,200 feet is perfectly acceptable for normal jumping on an open airfield. Once the pilot has lined up the aircraft downwind of the cross it is up to you to guide him over it bearing in mind that he cannot see directly below the aircraft unless he banks it over. In your briefing (especially if the pilot is new to the game), you should stress the importance of keeping the aircraft turns as flat as possible using the rudder with a touch of opposite aileron; if the turns are banked (as in normal flying) you will not be looking straight down when you are lining up the aircraft. Be wary of using the sill of the door as a guide to line up the aircraft as quite often it will not be running directly fore and aft, but at an angle. Occasionally drift will upset your accuracy in this respect as although the nose of the aircraft is pointing towards the cross the upper wind is tending to move it crab-like away to one side of it. It is easiest if you have a system of lights to signal your directions to the pilot or if he can see your handsignals in a mirror, but shouting direction is perfectly acceptable if carried out correctly; first

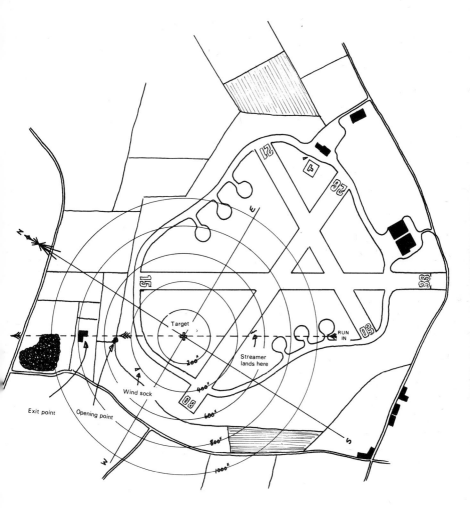

Fig. 26. Typical airfield with DZ layout. Arrowed broken line shows the run-in for this example.

give the direction, then the number of degrees, i.e. 'Right...five' or 'Left...ten'. Having given the correction let the aircraft settle on its new heading; if you do not allow this to happen and give the pilot a continuous flow of corrections, not only will your spot be inaccurate but the pilot will immediately be aware of your inexperience and shouldn't be blamed if he starts to ignore you! When you are directly over the target cross you can throw the streamer; remember, however, that if the aircraft is still climbing there will be a tendency for you to be looking ahead and not straight down, the converse being true if the aircraft is descending. Just before throwing the streamer you should unroll the first two or three feet and retain this amount in your grip; this will ensure that it unrolls immediately it is thrown into the slipstream. The moment is now right so throw the streamer violently outwards and downwards, shouting 'OKAY...' which is an immediate signal for the pilot to *bank* the aircraft hard around to the side from which you have thrown it. Ideally it is best to time the streamer's descent using a stopwatch and it should take about 100 seconds. Once you have thrown the streamer don't take your eyes off it until it reaches the ground; it is very easy to lose sight of a streamer in hazy conditions or when it's descending against a non-contrasting background. Now it is a simple matter to mark where the streamer landed on the airphotograph with a chinagraph pencil; then using a small ruler draw a line through the point where the streamer landed, through the target cross and beyond. The distance between these two points marked on the straight line on the other side of the target cross will give you the opening point–see Figure 26. The airphotographs can now be passed to the pilot and the other jumpers in the aircraft. If you do not have an airphotograph then the process should be done visually, giving the pilot and other jumpers the opening point in relation to prominent features or landmarks on the ground. So far we have only determined our canopy drift but the wind will also effect us in free fall and this must be the next consideration.

The first thing to remember when calculating how far you will drift during the free fall phase of the descent is that two knots equal one metre per second. The reason for knowing this is that pilots talk of speed in knots and when you obtain wind speeds from Met. Offices they will also be given in knots. In practise jumpers seldom calculate their free fall drift but tend to guess at it by looking at the upper clouds or by just making a correction after the first aircraft load of the day have landed off the airfield. For casual club jumping this may be acceptable but you must know how to calculate free fall drift accurately for the occasion when you are jumping into a restricted drop zone from, say, 10,000 feet and when tracking to the opening point is not what you have planned for the free fall phase of the descent. First you must obtain an accurate Met. wind forecast and your pilot will advise you as to the nearest Met. Office, (in some cases you may have to book your requirements in advance). The information that you receive should be tabulated as in the example given below:

Height in Feet		Speed		Direction (from which the wind is coming in degrees true)
		knots	metres/sec	
Canopy Drift	Surface	8	4	260°
	1,000	10	5	270°
	2,000	12	6	270°
Free Fall Drift	3,000	16	8	280°
	4,000	18	9	280°
	5,000	22	11	290°
	6,000	28	14	310°
	7,000	30	15	320°
	8,000	36	18	340°
	9,000	40	20	340°
	10,000	40	20	350°
		8 $\backslash$ 115		8 $\backslash$ 2510
		$14\frac{1}{2}$		314

To calculate free fall drift simply add up the free fall drift wind speed in metres and the wind direction in degrees; in this case 115 and 2510. To find the average now divide each of these totals by the number of sets of figures, in this case 8, and we get $14\frac{1}{2}$ metres per second and 314 degrees. This simply means that for every second of free fall the drift is $14\frac{1}{2}$ metres from a direction of 314 degrees. In this case we have fifty seconds of free fall (see the chart at the end of this chapter), therefore the total drift is $14\frac{1}{2} \times 50$ metres or 715 metres. This distance of 715 and direction of 314 degrees can now be plotted on the airphotograph to provide the exit point. Additionally, your canopy drift can be calculated from the figures given above and occasionally this is necessary when jumping at an airshow or the like where a tight schedule does not allow for the throwing of a streamer. The procedure is the same, simply average out the three sets of figures bracketed as canopy drift and you get a result of 5 metres/sec from 267 degrees. You will be hanging under your canopy for about two minutes, therefore 5 metres per second for 120 seconds gives a canopy drift of 600 metres. Here again this can be plotted on the airphotograph to provide the opening point.

The final consideration is that of the throw forward and more often than not it is ignored but once in a while the occasion will arise when it is of paramount importance. Two examples of this are first when accuracy jumping on a virtually nil wind condition day when it may be necessary to exit downwind of the target cross to allow for the throw forward to the pre-determined opening point upwind, and secondly when jumping from an aircraft with a much higher run in speed than normally experienced. Throw forward is calculated by using the formula $P = \frac{VT}{T+5}$ where P is the required throw forward in metres, V is the True Air Speed of the aircraft in metres per second and T is the lenght of delay in seconds up to a maximum of twelve seconds (terminal velocity). An example of this might be jumping from a Cessna 172 with a True Air Speed of 65 knots (32 metres per second) on a ten second delay.

$$P = \frac{5 \times 32 \times 10}{10+5} = \frac{\cancel{5} \times 32 \times 10}{\cancel{15}_3} = \frac{320}{3}$$
$$= 107 \text{ metres}$$

The exit point on the airphotograph can now be adjusted accordingly. The only catch here is that True Air Speed increases with altitude and decreases with lowering of temperature, e.g. a True Air Speed of 37 metres per second at 3,000 feet and 0° Centigrade will become 40 metres per second at 10,000 feet and —10° Centigrade – complicated? I agree, so we'll ignore it!

You will be introduced to spotting during Category VII and this is simply done by your having a go at it with your instructor looking over your shoulder and guiding you as necessary. Once again, only practice makes perfect and you will probably find that to spot consistently accurately is a little more difficult than you had at first anticipated, so take a pride in this neglected art.

DISTANCE FALLEN IN FREE FALL STABLE SPREAD POSITION
THIS TABLE IS COMPUTED FOR FREE FALL IN THE STABLE SPREAD (FACE TO EARTH) POSITION, FOR AN OPENING

ALTITUDE OF 2,000 FEET ABOVE SEA LEVEL AND FOR AVERAGE SUMMER TEMPERATURES AND PRESSURE CONDITIONS.

CAUTION: The rate of descent increases with (1) other body position, (2) higher temperatures, (3) lower pressure (e.g. higher field elevation). Use this table with extreme caution at field elevations over 1,000 feet, especially during long delays. Always add 100 feet extra for each 1,000 feet of field elevation.

Distance Fallen each Second to Terminal Velocity		Total Distance Fallen in Free Fall Stable Spread Position Distance Measured in Feet.			
Secs.	Distance	Secs.	Distance	Secs.	Distance
1	16	1	16	13	1657
2	46	2	62	14	1831
3	76	3	138	15	2005
4	104	4	242	16	2179
5	124	5	366	17	2353
6	138	6	504	18	2527
7	148	7	652	19	2701
8	156	8	808	20	2875
9	163	9	971	21	3049
10	167	10	1138	22	3223
11	171	11	1309	23	3397
12	174	12	1483	24	3571

Total Distance Fallen in Free Fall Stable Spread Position (cont.)

Secs.	Distance	Secs.	Distance	Secs.	Distance
25	3745	37	5833	49	7921
26	3919	38	6007	50	8095
27	4093	39	6181	51	8269
28	4267	40	6355	52	8443
29	4441	41	6529	53	8617
30	4615	42	6703	54	8791
31	4789	43	6877	55	8965
32	4963	44	7051	56	9139
33	5137	45	7225	57	9313
34	5311	46	7399	58	9487
35	5485	47	7573	59	9661
36	5659	48	7747	60	9835

As an example, if a 20 second delay is required, look up the distance fallen against 20 seconds (in this case 2875) and add the normal opening height of 2,000 feet; this gives 4875 feet or 5,000 feet in round figures.

Chapter 14

Relative Work and Camera Jumping

Relative work may be defined as the ability two or more parachutists have to move under control relative to one another in free fall so that they may pass a baton from one to another, link up or, if the parachutist's companion is of the opposite sex, execute a lipstick pass (sorry, but sex had to come into this book sooner or later!) Relative work is a branch of sport parachuting that has tended to lag behind style or accuracy because a parachutist cannot perform it solo, and in its infancy it tended to be a dangerous hit-and-miss affair. It has now become an exact aerodynamic science which probably imparts to man the nearest equivalent to actually flying like a bird that there is.

The two principal dangers of relative work are first, the possibility of taking altitude for granted having become too engrossed in the task you have set yourself, and secondly, the two kinds of collision. Both kinds of collision could have disastrous results; the free fall collision (where closing speeds of up to 100 mph could occur), possibly resulting in unconsciousness, and the canopy collision (normally at or just after opening time), possibly resulting in one or both canopies malfunctioning. Therefore you can see that you must have a good deal of experience before starting relative work and this is why it is not introduced until Category IX. You must have complete control of your body in free fall and know the bodily effects of basic limb movements; you must also be able to track proficiently.

Because of the potential dangers it is essential that your first few relative work jumps are carried out with a jumper who has a sound working knowledge of the subject, preferably an instructor. (Although one of the instructor qualifications is the requirement to be a Category X parachutist, i.e. one who has been cleared for relative parachuting, it is amazing how many instructors are incapable of relative work themselves, let alone of teaching it!) Apart from the dangers of experimenting with one of your friends from student days, you are wasting time and money by not having a proper grounding in the subject; so when you choose your relative work tutor, ensure that he has plenty of experience and the ability to pass it on to you.

Any relative work jump should be carefully pre-planned but the briefings for your first half dozen or so must be clear and comprehensive. Your instructor will tell you first what he wants *you* to do, next what he is going to do himself, thirdly the particular points he wants you to look out for, and finally the wave off height and procedure. Your instructor will tell you also the problems you will individually encounter because of your size and weight. If you are heavy (over about 13 stone) or thick-set in build, you can expect that your free fall rate of descent relative to the average will be high and conversely if you are a lightweight (less than about 11 stone) or are gangly in build, you can expect a lower relative free fall rate of descent. There is no official policy of relative work progression but the following suggested programme for the first half dozen jumps has worked well for me when teaching beginners; I hope it will for you. Remember, any jump that does not go according to plan should be repeated until it does.

Jump No. 1 (from over 7,500 feet)

The student relative worker will exit the aircraft first on the instructor's word and assume a full spread position (for slowest free fall rate of descent) on a given heading, which will normally be that of the aircraft. He will look up and watch the instructor exit behind him, being careful not to have his head thrown too far back as this will cause him to backslide away from the instructor. He will be told to watch the instructor's initial reduction which will be done by adopting a gentle delta position aiming just slightly to one side of the student. The student will then note the method of flaring out by the instructor to a full spread position, ideally about twenty feet above and forty feet straight out from him. From here the student should notice the instructor's use of full arm movements to achieve a final position about four to six feet away and on the same level. If the student is in a relaxed, constant stable position which does not cause him to jostle about the sky relative to the instructor, the latter may well close this gap and make a final link-up by grasping the student's wrists, but this final closing is not vital for the first descent. When wave off height arrives, if they are not linked the instructor will wave off by giving windscreen-wiper type movements in front of his face and if they are linked, the instructor will simply break it. The student will then observe the instructor's right turn through 180° before tracking away for canopy deployment by them both at 2,000 feet. If the student can turn slightly away from the instructor's line of track, this will completely eliminate canopy collision. Remember that high performance canopies have the characteristics of surging forward during deployment and any jumpers in a group at opening height should be facing outwards.

Jump No. 2 (from over 7,500 feet)
This jump is the same as No.1 with the exception that the student is carefully briefed to watch the final few feet of the instructor's approach to the link-up. The final few feet of closing is the most critical part of relative work and will inevitably be the most difficult to perfect. The student must watch the movements of the instructor's hands noting how he has them palms downwards, with a bending at the elbows to achieve forward movement. If the final closing is too fast, forward speed will be reduced by letting the hands ride up so that the palms are facing forwards. There should be no attempt at a last-minute grabbing of the wrists as any violent movement at this stage will certainly cause momentary instability which will prevent a smooth link. If the student is completely clear on the wave-off procedure after the first jump he will be allowed to practise the 180° right turn and track to opening with the instructor also moving away but at a slight angle so that he can observe the student's performance.

Jump No. 3 (from over 7,500 feet)
The exit order is the same as for the previous two jumps and the aim of this jump is to practise the student in the final closing to the link. The instructor will descend to the student's level and, instead of setting up for the final closing about four to six feet directly in front of him, will set himself up at about 90° to the student's heading, about four to six feet to one side. The student (on being given a thumbs up or previously agreed sign) will then turn towards his instructor and close the gap for the link. On this jump it should be the student's job to initiate the wave off and on the performance of this vital action the instructor will be very critical.

Jump No. 4 (from over 7,500 feet)
The exit order is now reversed with the instructor exiting first and stabilising on a heading of his choosing. The student will then practise the reduction, approach and final closing to the link before initiating wave-off at the correct height.

Jump No. 5 (from over 7,500 feet)

The initial part of this jump is the same as jump No. 4 but after the link the instuctor will give a nod as a signal for both he and the student to break, execute a 360° turn to the right and link again. (The instructor will do none of the final closing movement himself, allowing the student to practise it himself). The wave-off and track for canopy deployment are as before.

Jump No. 6 (from above 10,000 feet)

The aim of this jump is for the student to participate in a three-man link-up and another experienced relative worker will be invited to come along as 'base' (or low) man. The student exits second as 'pin' man (i.e. to pin the base man). Once the student links with the base man the instructor will move in and form the three-man. The student will be briefed on the necessity of flying the base as tightly as possible, i.e. with the elbows tucked in so that base man and pin man are almost helmet to helmet; this is important as a loose link will not be as stable and will also have more lift, making final closure by the third man more difficult. Also it can be seen that the base must remain on the same heading; it is virtually impossible to link with a rotating base. Once he has closed, the instructor will demonstrate how to grip the forearms of base man and pin man and how he must physically break apart their grip to avoid premature break up of the link; this is a basic principle of larger link-ups and star work, of which more later.

Having achieved this basic grounding, the budding relative worker should continue to improve his knowledge by working with jumpers of different weights and experience. But before going on to discuss the fascinating art of star work, a few general tips are now given to fill any gaps that have arisen so far.

'Take not thine altitude in vain, for the earth shall arise and smite thee'; this commandment is more relevant in relative work than in other branches of the sport because of the obvious dangers of becoming engrossed in making the link or whatever. Normally the base man is responsible for keeping an eye on the altitude but having said that, it is also each individual's responsibility as part of his make-up of being a safe sport parachutist. It takes but a second to glance at your altimeter anyway. In this connection, wave off height should not be below 3,500 feet but obviously may be more during your early relative jumps. Safety must always be uppermost in your mind and if things are not going according to plan, ensure that the danger is not increased; a few examples are given. If you think you are going to hit a link too fast and possibly cause it to break, move off to one side; if a three-man is having stability problems, don't move in until they are completely under control; if you're base man and the eighth man is just closing to make your first eight-man star at 3,500, don't be tempted to wait a couple more seconds to give the wave-off–it may be the last decision you make! Bear in mind that it is not easy to lose the reputation of being a dangerous sport parachutist, and if you have this kind of reputation you should not be surprised if your friends have a distinct reluctance to jump with you.

Fast exits are important in relative work and a good dive exit without touching the door can be achieved without much practice. With this jostling for a fast exit going on in the aircraft there is an increased danger of premature reserve deployment, but it is a simple matter to keep one hand on the reserve handle until you reach the door.

During relative work the spot is not important (providing there is plenty of open space where you can touch down) and therefore, at wave-off time it is essential that everyone turns right through 180° and tracks away. Don't be tempted to track for the opening point you have used on a previous accuracy jump–this is a sure way to cause a free fall collision. The moment your canopy is deployed, grasp the toggles as you may need to steer quickly to avoid a canopy collision, then have a good look round and see where the other jumpers are positioned. Now if you are in a good position to have a go at the target, fair enough, but keep your eyes open and don't be too proud to give way to the idiot who has his eyes glued on the target cross even if he is higher than you; (if he's lower than you he has right of way anyway). Remember that this is a relative jump and not an accuracy contest.

Once on the ground ensure that you all get together for a comprehensive debrief because if you don't bother, much of the value of the jump will be wasted. If you've made a mistake–admit it; you'll be respected more by your fellow jumpers than the character who continually tries to blame others and even the best relative workers make a booby now and then.

Star Relative Work

I shall now discuss the fascinating business of building stars. Pioneered in the USA, star relative work has developed to being an aerodynamic science of dedicated team work. With sixty seconds of relative work time from 12,500 feet, it might seem that there is a limit to the size of star that can be built at the time of writing a 31-man star is the world record – one which no doubt will not remain unbroken for very long. In America the star has been defined as an eight-man or better; if you want to call your six-man a star then go ahead, but when you finally make an eight-man you'll probably agree with this definition!

Organisation is the first requirement and ideally one man should be responsible for getting the team together on the drop zone, deciding the exit order and running the important pre-jump and post-jump briefings. Exit order should be primarily determined by individuals' weight but experience may also have to be considered. The heavy men in the team should exit first with the lightweight bringing up the rear, and each man being given alternately left and right as his particular side from which to approach the group. Jumpers in star work must be picked for their ability and even if an apparently experienced jumper, who keeps making the same mistakes, is not replaced, your star simply will not happen. Successful star work is more a result of satisfactory team work than any other branch of the sport, and the leader may even have the thankless task of replacing a close friend to achieve this result.

Aircraft will inevitably pose a problem. Without a doubt the remarkable Short Skyvan is ideal for relative work, and because of its suitability for this role, rather than for other types of sport parachuting, it was not mentioned in Chapter 5. It will lift fifteen parachutists to heights in excess of 10,000 feet within ten to twelve minutes, and has a tailgate type of door which provides for very fast exits. Regrettably, they are not readily available, and unless you can produce a DC3 (Dakota), or similar sized aircraft, you will certainly be forced into using two or more smaller aircraft. Actually this is not a major difficulty as the aircraft do not have to fly in tight formation, but in a loose line diagonally back to left or right from the lead aircraft.

Having exited the aircraft, the first essential requirement is the forming of a fast, stable base. Normally the two heaviest jumpers on the load are the 'pin' and 'base' men and should, with practice, be able to link sub-terminally. Having got together they should fly the base as tightly as possible (legs tucked in, helmet to helmet) and ensure that it remains on heading. The base man has the additional responsibility of being No.1 height watching man. Don't fall into the temptation of using a base man of limited experience – if the base men don't get together, or make a mess of it when they do, you're wasting your time.

Fast exits are obviously very desirable and the lightweights at the back

Andy Keech

Build up to a large star

of the load should exit in a dive and hold a full head down delta position aiming for the group. As the group is approached, the lightweights can ease off their speed by widening the delta to flare out and to position themselves level with the star and about twenty feet out. Later this approach can be refined to bringing the jumper into a final closing position just above the heels of the jumpers already in the star, but the dangers of practising this technique right away are obvious. Each individual should have a pre-determined 'slot' in the star.

If a jumper drops beneath the star he can often get up again, especially if he is a lightweight. The required technique is called 'de-arching'; the jumper should look up to ensure he is well to one side of the star, then he should look down at the ground, round his back and push his extended arms and legs to a full reverse arch position. The effect is often surprising as the jumper appears to pop up like a cork out of a bottle relative to the star. It is a useful salvaging technique to give the jumper another chance for a final approach.

At this time it may well be that the star is turning or wobbling slightly, and the final approach into the slot should be checked until the star has settled. This is also a chance to have a quick look to see that no one else is lining up for the same slot. Once having arrived at his slot the jumper is faced with the actual entry which is the most difficult part of the jump. When the star builds up to more than a four-man, turbulence is building up proportionately and this turbulence (or 'burble') must be broken through. If the jumper's forward speed is insufficient he simply will not break through the burble and, of course, if his forward speed is excessive there is a risk of busting the star apart. The forward speed of entry is therefore critical. Lightweights normally find it easiest to enter the last metre from a slightly lower level than the star relying on the burble to 'lift' them into the slot, and heavyweights conversely tend to come in from a slightly higher level. Reaching for the wrists in the relevant slot will tend to give additional lift, especially for lightweights. As the jumper actually grasps the wrists (or handful of jumpsuit) he must simultaneously tuck forward his legs; if this is not done the extra lift given to the legs will cause a forward somersault in towards the centre of the star, which will inevitably break it up.

The grip is most important as a weak one can so easily wreck a star once it is lost. The golden rule, therefore, is that the two jumpers on either side of the slot do not relax their grip until it is physically broken by being forced apart by the jumper entering that particular slot. As

Lou Johnson

Sally Williams demonstrates the need for a good grip before breaking into
a star

each jumper enters the star his job is not yet finished, for each must concentrate on 'flying' the star to enable it to remain flat and stable. Basically each should try to fall level to the jumper opposite him by varying the amount of tucking of his arms and legs. Flying the star is not as easy as it sounds and will only come with practice. Finally the wave off is exactly as previously described with the base man shaking away from the two jumpers on either side of him as a sign for everyone to turn to the right through 180° and track for canopy deployment. Once on the ground, all must gather together for a comprehensive debrief to ensure that mistakes are not repeated on future jumps.

The more refined details of building stars will be best found out by experience but the tips given above will provide you with a basic grounding.

Camera Jumping

Sooner or later you may well wish to record the excitement of the sport on film and the idea of camera jumping will rear its ugly head. I say 'ugly head' as when a novice camera jumper sets out on his photographic adventure he is not normally aware of the pitfalls that await him. The aim of this part of the chapter is not to go into elaborate detail but rather to give general tips which will assist the novice cameraman in avoiding some of these pitfalls.

Two basic requirements are immediately obvious: first a sound grounding in relative work, and secondly a fair knowledge of photography. Assuming you have these requirements you must decide whether you wish to shoot stills or cine. I recommend stills initially as the cost of experimenting is considerably less than with cine.

Many camera jumpers start off with a wrist-mounted set-up and it has a number of advantages: the sighting is easy, the film may be wound on manually and the mount itself is relatively simple to make; but the wrist-mount has one major disadvantage: you're like a bird without wings for every time you take a photo your hands are drawn across the front of your face with obvious results. The camera must, therefore, be mounted on your helmet to allow you full use of your arms.

Bearing this in mind, you now come to the choice of camera and you should be immediately aware of the need for some sort of motor drive as you cannot wind on the film manually when helmet-mounted. I strongly advise that you go for full frame 35mm for best reproduction in case you get a saleable photograph (this angle should always be

The author models his helmet-mounted motorised Nikon F camera used to take many of the air to air free fall photographs in this book.

considered as it could pay for a few jumps or even your camera!) The camera should have shutter speeds to at least 1/500 of a second and a semi-wide angle lens with a focal length of about 35mm. You should be able to find something to suit your pocket from the Ricoh and Leningrad types (about £50 each) to the sophistication of the motorised

Nikon at about £350; here you may be guided by your local photo-graphic dealer who will probably show a good deal of interest when you tell him to what use you intend to put it.

If you have a professional do the job of mounting the camera on your helmet then you've no problem, but doing the job yourself is not too difficult and can be very rewarding. Initially make a mock-up mount using thin card and with this shape as a template you can cut out the $\frac{1}{16}''$ steel or $\frac{1}{8}''$ aluminium sheet. Once the sheet material is cut you may need professional help to shape and weld or rivet it. Be careful when drilling holes in the fibreglass of the helmet as it can crack and make sure you use large washers on the securing bolts on the inside for the same reason. Three final points on the design of the mount: first try to have two separate methods of securing the camera to the mount (the normal tripod bush at the base is not usually strong enough on its own); secondly the mount wants to be as close to the helmet as possible for easier balance, and finally make sure the intricacies of the mount do not interfere with the working parts of the camera.

Two types of shutter release should be considered, either the standard mechanical cable release or an electrical system using a solenoid. Avoid the bulb releases with the length of rubber tubing as change of pressure with altitude plays havoc with them. The sighting is usually done using a polaroid bullseye sight (with Newton's rings), but other methods may be used providing they are carefully zeroed with the viewfinder of the camera.

Whatever design you decide on, however, it will be well worth your while to have a chat with an established camera jumper for advice; I can't think of any who wouldn't gladly pass on any help or samples of their experience if asked. The problems of choosing and mounting cine cameras are similar; go for fifty-foot magazine load 16mm with an electric motor. The choice is not so varied but the American surplus AN-N2 may be obtained fairly cheaply and produces acceptable results. You can now set up the camera for the jump and a fast film is needed to allow at least 1/500 second shutter speed (or 32 frames/sec on cine) at a stop of f.11 or f.16 for maximum depth of focus (you can't alter the focus once you've left the aircraft!) Check the camera carefully and shoot a frame or two to make sure it is working. Choose a bright day and one with a few fluffy white cumulus clouds as background (a yellow filter will accentuate these on black and white film). Light, bright coloured jumpsuits make for crisp pictures (black is a miserable colour for free fall photography), and try to jump well before or well after midday as the sun is then lower in the sky.

Your first jump should be with only one subject and it's advisable for you to exit first and let your subject get down to you—you have quite enough extra problems on the first camera jump. Always choose subjects who are 100% reliable as you tend to have to rely on them for wave off; too many cameramen have been scared too often on photographic jumps and although it's fairly easy to sneak a glance at an altimeter with a still camera, it's a different matter with cine as every movement of the head is reflected on film. I cannot stress enough the importance of pre-planning the jump and wave off procedure; vain parachutists have caught me out a couple of times and it isn't very funny. After wave off, one hand placed on the helmet during the pull will reduce the head whip experienced during canopy deployment until your muscles become used to the idea.

Finally, it must be pointed out that parachutists tend to be a vain lot and once you're established as a camera jumper they will have you performing in this capacity at every available opportunity. Do not be pushed into camera jumping in tricky conditions; bear in mind that you have an additional variable with which to cope and it's your head!

Chapter 15

Competition Parachuting

In 1951, five nations met in Yugoslavia for a parachuting competition which was, in essence, the first World Championships, but it was not until the Second World Championships were held at St. Yan in France in 1954 that the Federation Aeronautique Internationale recognised parachuting as a sport. Since then the FAI have arranged the World Championships, held every other year as follows: 1956–Tushino, Russia; 1958–Bratislavia, Czechoslovakia; 1960–Sofia, Bulgaria; 1962–Orange, USA; 1964–Leutkirch, West Germany; 1966–Leipzig, East Germany; 1968–Gtaz, Austria; 1970–Bled, Yugoslavia; 1972–Talequah, USA; 1974–Szolnok, Hungary. In these twenty years parachuting has developed from a seemingly hazardous outdoor activity to become a rational sport in which its participants compete with utmost skill and chivalrous rivalry to become individual champions or to gain athletic honour for their country.

Participation in competition parachuting can be divided into two types. You can either compete to enjoy another branch of the sport, knowing that you'll never achieve top honours but enjoying it for the relaxation, friendly rivalry and the gaining of further parachuting knowledge that always comes about when jumpers gather together in competition; or you can compete to win and prove your skill. Probably most parachutists are of the first type because they haven't the wholehearted patience, dedication and self-discipline that is required of a top-line competition jumper. You cannot expect to represent your country or to achieve top honours without a good deal of frustration and single-minded determination, but nevertheless the satisfaction of success may well be ample reward.

Although parachute competitions can take many different forms (and here the not-so-expert parachutist can enjoy the invention and participation in novel types of competition), the only types of event that are

157

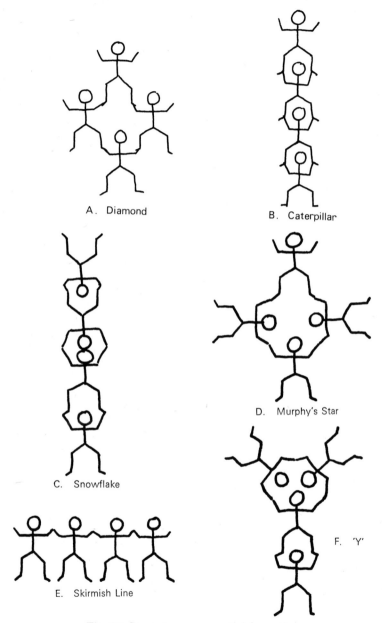

A. Diamond

B. Caterpillar

C. Snowflake

D. Murphy's Star

E. Skirmish Line

F. 'Y'

Fig. 27. Some 4-man sequential formations.

currently used in World competition are those of 'style', 'accuracy' and 'relative work'.

Style is an individual event only and the competitor is judged solely on his ability to perform fast, precise manoeuvres whilst in free fall. Accuracy may be an individual or team event where ability to control the parachute canopy will be of prime importance, to enable the parachutist to land as close as possible to a given spot on the ground.

Relative work has two competitive events and these are the 10-Man Speed Star and the 4-Man Sequential. In the first the emphasis is on speed of building a 10-Man Star, and in the second the time is taken after an initial 4-Man has been broken to the time a second formation has been put together.

Throughout the remainder of this chapter I will endeavour to confine myself to providing you with the basic format of these events and a number of coaching tips to give you an initial grounding in the skills required. It is not my intention to go into the more detailed rules of the game as these tend to change slightly from year to year. The detailed reading and interpretation of rules are a very important part of the preparation for any competition, and will often result in a welcome re-jump or the reversal of a judge's decision.

Style

Style jumps are made from 1,800 to 2,000 metres (5,900 feet – 6,600 feet) depending on local rules. This allows approximately between 22 and 27 seconds to exit the aircraft, build up to terminal velocity, align with the heading arrow on the ground and perform the six manoeuvres of the style series, before opening the canopy at 2,000 feet. The basic rules of style are straightforward. Competitors will normally each perform three jumps (which form the three rounds of the event) and they will each perform the same series in any one round; the three style series being:

First Group (Left Series) – Left Turn, Right Turn, Back Loop, Left Turn, Right Turn, Back Loop.

Second Group (Right Series) – Right Turn, Left Turn, Back Loop, Right Turn, Left Turn, Back Loop.

Third Group (Cross Series) – Left Turn, Right Turn, Back Loop, Right Turn, Left Turn, Back Loop.

Positioned on the ground will be the huge white heading arrow which can be readily seen from jump height. As accuracy plays no part in style the parachutist is given a pre-determined exit point by the judges which they choose for their ease of viewing each jumper's performance through telemeters (large binoculars). After exit from the aircraft, terminal velocity should be achieved before the competitor starts the series in order to avoid the sloppiness of sub-terminal manoeuvre. During this build-up to terminal velocity the competitor should line up precisely with the heading arrow before spinning into the first turn. Style is judged on two features, speed and precision. Each manoeuvre must be carried out as fast as possible but with complete precision so that each turn and loop is completed with the jumper on heading with the arrow. Penalty points are deducted for undershooting and overshooting turns (the exact number of penalty points varying with the degree of overshoot and undershoot), rolling off loops or failing to complete them on heading and for carrying out manoeuvres with the body inclined off a vertical axis. Loss of all points will occur if the parachutist performs the wrong series, omits any manoeuvre of the correct series, or performs additional manoeuvres to those prescribed for that particular series.

When you start style jumping you should concentrate initially on precision (or turning a 'clean' series), rather than on speed. Once you can turn a well co-ordinated clean series you can then start to cut down on the time. In theory it has been calculated that the minimum time for each manoeuvre is ·8 to ·9 of a second, which gives a total theoretical time of 4·8 to 5·4 seconds, but of course this assumes perfect performance and no time gap between each manoeuvre. There is a sub-conscious tendency when starting style to practise one particular series and the mistake of doing this is obvious, so write up each successive style jump in your log book, showing its type and time, together with relevant criticisms. If you can have a friend observing you either from the ground with binoculars or in free fall, so much the better as you're more likely to learn from someone else's critique than from one which is self-administered.

Accuracy

Accuracy jumps are made from 600 to 1,000 metres (2,200 to 3,200 feet) depending on local rules. Where there is a jump altitude of 3,000 feet the competitor has the flexibility of opening between nought and ten seconds after exit which means that he can alter his length of time under the canopy to adjust the spot if necessary. The number of accuracy jumps in a competition may vary but four has become a usual figure which sometimes allows for the lowest score of the four to be ignored or 'thrown away'. The 'target area' is a circular pit of fine pea gravel at least thirty metres in diameter. The 'dead centre' of the target area (or DC) is marked with an orange fluorescent disc, normally fifteen centimetres in diameter (it may be ten centimetres in international competition). The inside ends of the four arms of the target cross are normally five metres from the disc. This allows a circle of ten metres in diameter of clear pea gravel with the disc in the centre. Distance of landing is measured to the nearest centimetre from dead centre and normal top-line competition scores 250 points for a dead centre. If the scoring area is a circle of ten metres radius, then 0·25 points are deducted for each centimetre away from dead centre and likewise if a 25 metre radius scoring area is required then 0·1 points will be deducted for each centimetre. The distance from DC is measured to the first point of bodily contact; for instance, if the disc is hit with the right foot but the trailing foot touches down first then it is to the left foot that the measurement is taken.

Before you actually emplane for an accuracy descent it is worth making a simple calculation to determine your 'attack point'. The attack point is an imaginary point on the ground over which you should be positioned at 100 metres of altitude (300 feet). Before you reach the attack point you can afford to zig-zag down the windline and, although it is untidy, even have your back to the target; but once you reach the attack point you must face downwind towards the target, only using small turning corrections to keep yourself precisely on the windline. The approximate distance of the attack point upwind from the disc along the windline is simply calculated by remembering that for every metre per second of wind speed you should be 25 metres out from the disc; i.e. in a five metre per second wind you should be 125 metres out from the disc at 100 metres of altitude ON HALF BRAKES. From the attack point to the ground you should not take your eyes off the disc for an instant and concentrate on gently increasing or decreasing the brakes depending on whether you are going to overshoot or undershoot the disc. It is important that you are precisely on the windline at the attack point otherwise you will have another variable to correct during this last critical twenty seconds of the descent. In the early stages of accuracy jumping you should once again make very gentle toggle corrections (in case you've grown out of the habit!); it is more important than ever for accuracy jumping that your canopy is completely stable for the last 300 feet to the disc. To aid vision you may find it helpful to lower one side of a chest mounted reserve and goggles should be raised as you may

A competitor in the Accuracy Event in the Army Championships on a MK I Para-commander, probably the world's most popular sport parachute.

Tony Jones shows good competition landing form—one foot leading, reserve dropped, goggles raised and both eyes on the disc.

get distortion otherwise. Some jumpers find it helpful to undo the chest strap; this tends to spread the canopy for a shade more glide and allows more freedom of the chest. The difference between a metre and a DC is made in that last and most difficult two seconds of the descent. Perfect control of the canopy must be retained to touch down so resist any temptation to let go of the toggles. Your heel (or heels) are the part of your body which ideally should strike first, and if you are only striking with one heel, make sure the other is tucked up out of the way. Beware of the dangers of not striking with the heel; two of the commonest are reaching with legs too much and landing on the base of the spine, or overshooting and reaching back, landing on your toes; both will inevitably be hospital jobs! The final reach with your heel for the disc is the key to success and grasping the rear risers will give you bodily reach which may well put you a metre closer. Avoid the tendency to strike always with the same foot as sooner or later it will strike just to one side of the disc while the other foot is immediately over it; reach for it with the most convenient foot. Any violent body movement in the harness will upset canopy trim so restrict your reach to the final second or two and only when it is absolutely necessary. Try to have an experienced jumper critique your approaches and landings and watching others perform is a sure way of learning accuracy techniques.

Team accuracy jumping presents one or two extra problems. A team usually consists of four jumpers and the openings should be 'stacked' up to avoid all four landing in the pit simultaneously. This can be done either visually or by timings. If the stack is effected visually, the first man exits the aircraft and opens on about eight seconds; each successive team member exits in turn and all pull when they see the low man pull. If timings are used each man opens after a pre-determined delay, i.e. the first (or low) man might pull on eight seconds, the second on six seconds, the third on four seconds, and the last (or high) man on two seconds. It is important that the weight of each jumper is considered; it may be that a heavy man out last may upset the stack or conversely it may be that a light man out last will be affected by winds above 2,500 feet that fail to affect those in the team whose canopies are open below this height. Perhaps the team leader wishes to exit first so that he can lead his team into the pit. The final point to remember about team jumping is to get out of the pit the moment you land in order that your team mates have a clear run and in order that the judges have unobstructed views. You can see, therefore, that team jumping will need extra planning before the event even though most of the problems will have been sorted out during practice.

Relative Work

The 10-Man Star event is probably the purest *team* event in sport parachuting, for if one man in the team fails to do his job properly it could mean a slow time or, worse still, just a 9-Man Star; and no major national or international 10-Man event will be won with 9-Mans!

The exit from the aircraft is very important for a split second at this stage will make seconds of difference clear of the aircraft. Current rules only allow a single file exit from the door with no jumper, or any of his equipment, showing outside the aircraft before the exit itself; and only

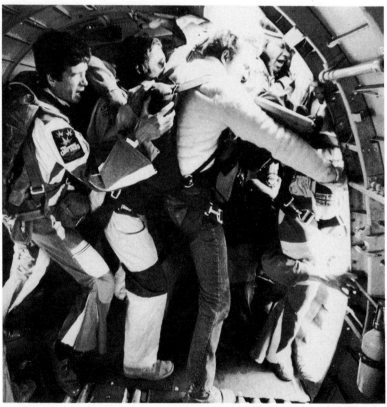

Dave Waterman
Only hours of practice on the ground will produce a slick fast exit

hours of practise on the ground will produce a slick fast exit, with every member of the team positioning himself in exactly the same place with the minimum of jostling. To aid the judging, the exit signal is normally from the ground so spotting will not be a problem.

The techniques for building fast stars can be argued indefinitely, but a system should be evolved which basically gives each team member the minimum distance to fly. It has been generally accepted that the use of 'floaters', (team members who exit the aircraft *before* the base and pin, and who 'float' back up relative to the base), will shorten the distance between the base pair and the back end of the team. Each team will evolve its own pattern, but it is essential that each individual goes to his pre-determined slot to cut out traffic problems.

The height for this event is 10,500 ft (3,200 metres), and the time is taken from exit of the first man to the instant the tenth breaks into the star, which must be held for 5 seconds. The normal working time being 40 seconds; any star built in a greater time fails to score.

Discussion, both before and after the jump, is most important and team members must learn to be self critical in order that mistakes are not repeated, and that techniques can be polished up. Team spirit is as much a requirement for success, as relative work ability, and to this end the moulding of ten individuals into a single workable unit is of utmost importance.

For the 4-Man sequential event, the jump altitude is normally 8,500 ft (2,500 metres). The speed of exit is not important, as there is no need to build the initial 4-Man sub-terminally; the reason being that maximum speed should be reached before starting the sequence in order to achieve fast manoeuvre. Once the 4-Man has been put together it is broken by each individual backlooping out of it–it is at this instant that the timing starts. The watches are stopped when the subsequent pre-allocated formation has been put together; this sequential formation must be held together for 5 seconds. Some of the 4-man sequential formations are shown in figure 27. Again it would be wrong to lay down any rules about the exact way the second formation is put together as the combinations are endless; only experimentation and practice will produce results in this event which is as much a test of relative work ability as the 10-Man speed star.

Judging
In all events judging will be conducted by a team of not normally less

than a chief judge and two assistants; additionally, extra help is required recording the scores and the recorder will be directed by the chief judge. Judging is a thankless task; style times have become so fast and accuracy so accurate that to produce precise results is far from easy. Inevitably the odd jumper will be disappointed in his score and blame the judges and, although each competitor has the right of protest (after payment of a suitable fee!), most of the dissension can be avoided by a comprehensive pre-competition briefing by the Chief Judge. If you have any doubt whatsoever about the rules you should query the Chief Judge at his briefing. Already video tape recordings of style are being used to simplify the judges' task and no doubt some electronic recording device will ultimately be used in accoracy, but until that time comes, try to respect the judges for the difficult job they have to do.

Training
Training for competition is not merely a question of easing up on the beer and knocking out a few style jumps the weekend beforehand. To be a top-line competition parachutist you must be physically very fit. I personally recommend running and circuit training for producing the best results, with the odd game of squash, or the like, to sharpen up your co-ordination. A modified stabilised harness is most useful for working on style and use of the trampoline has been found to be beneficial also. Ground training is probably the tedious part of preparing for competition, but as you achieve physical fitness the sense of well-being you have will outweigh the purgatory of actually getting fit. The most difficult problem to some parachutists is the mental preparation; parachutists have been known to produce excellent results in practice but competition nerves on the day have forced disastrous results. The secret to success is to be sufficiently relaxed and the right mental attitude will help you achieve it if this is your problem. It may help if you positively try to enjoy the competition rather than to win and never lose your temper after a bad jump; hurling your helmet in disgust at the nearest judge will do no one any good, least of all you.
In the end, however, dedication and determination will make you a competition jumper; the best of luck!

Chapter 16

Display Jumping

Sooner or later you will be asked to participate in a parachute display for the public's entertainment and in so doing you will experience another branch of the sport which has its own appeal and its own pitfalls for the unwary. The first two paragraphs of the BPA rules on displays are worth quoting in full:

"1. All display parachutists and particularly Instructors and Jump-masters who accept the responsibility for giving parachute displays must take into account the risks and possible consequences of displays which misfire. Sound judgement should NEVER be influenced by the desire not to disappoint the organisers and the public. Injuries sustained in public and parachutists who land outside the arena have an adverse effect on responsible opinion since they usually result from incompetence or jumping in un-suitable conditions.

    Display parachuting calls for the highest standards of planning, co-ordination, experience, mutual confidence, safety-conscious-ness and parachuting skill. For these reasons parachutists who cannot be relied upon to do what is expected of them should not be permitted to take part in displays."

Let us examine the display in chronological order of events bearing in mind that the planning of the display itself will undoubtedly be reflected in the final result.

Having received the initial inquiry from the show organiser you should arrange to meet him on the actual site for the display about six weeks before the event. You should arm yourself with a 1″ to one mile Ordnance Survey map of the area, the Northern or Southern Aeronau-tical Chart ICAO 1:500,000 (available from your local flying club), together with paper and pencil. The show organisers should be asked to produce a 6″ to one mile map of the show ground and its surrounding

areas and, if there is any difficulty over this, advise them to approach
the local borough surveyor for a photostat copy. The organiser may
well have some preconceived ideas about the capabilities of your team
and you should immediately point out your limitations and how wind
and cloud may affect your display on the day. Overshoot areas are very
important as they can allow a certain margin of error; they should be
considered in the light of the prevailing wind, but of course, even this
may change on the day and the DZ should be examined in this light.
Paragraph 6 of Section XXI of BPA Regulations is quoted in full but
remember that a 75 yard diameter DZ with plenty of open space all
around it could easily be a much safer proposition than a 150 yard
diameter DZ with poor overshoot areas:

"6. *RESTRICTED DZs*

(*a*) Parachutists with not fewer than 200 Free Fall descents may
give displays using DZs of not less than 75 yards diameter, which
are free of major hazards and providing not more than 10% of this
area is taken up with minor hazards. In all such cases, however,
adequate overshoot areas must exist on all sides.

(*b*) 'C' Licence holders with not less than 100 descents may give
demonstrations on to DZs of not less than 150 yards diameter
providing that:

(1) They are approved for such demonstrations on to Restricted
DZs by their Club CIs.

(2) They are approved for each such demonstration by an
Instructor with knowledge of their ability as demonstration
parachutists and of the DZ in question.

(3) The aircraft is carrying a Jumpmaster who is a **BPA**
Instructor holding a 'D' Certificate.

(4) There are adequate overshoot areas on at least three sides
of the DZ."

The most difficult part of your planning visit to the display drop zone
is to imagine how it will look on the day with car parks, marquees and
sideshows filling your carefully chosen overshoot areas to capacity.
This problem should be fully discussed with the show organiser and all
these hazards should be marked accurately on the 6″ to one mile plan
of the showground. You can then check the Aeronautical Chart to see
if the DZ lies in controlled airspace or under an airway, and possibly
tell the organiser of any problem that there might be in this respect.
(If you have any doubt on this, a quick 'phone call to the relevant

office of the Civil Aviation Authority will provide the answer.) Sometimes it is very difficult to refuse an enthusiastic show organiser his display for a perfectly valid reason which he may not fully understand, but if you have the slightest doubt about its feasibility you should take this course of action.

Having agreed to undertake the display, however, you can now discuss the exact details of the event with the organisers. The financial side of it should be tied up with a written agreement based on aircraft flying time at £'x' per hour, cost per individual parachutist and a cancellation fee in case of bad weather. It is best to give a quote to the organiser which will not be exceeded and it should be pointed out that in addition to the cancellation fee there could be some aircraft positioning to pay for. £10 per parachutist is a reasonable fee for the average part-time team and £10 a fair cancellation fee; these figures are only given as a guide but don't fleece the organisers financially, otherwise you are unlikely to have them engage you the following year. At the mention of cancellation fees some organisers will visibly show their disapproval but you should point out that free fall displays are always a good crowd draw and that the crowd will normally have paid their gate money well before the display is cancelled unless it is a really terrible day for the weather.

You can now discuss the timings for the display and here it is helpful to point out that the weather tends to be better for parachuting later in the day and, of course, the later the display is scheduled the longer the crowd is kept in the showground. If you are doing more than one display on the same day you should allow plenty of time for repacking and travelling to the mounting airfield. Another useful point worth mentioning to the organiser is that having picked a time for the display he should try to stick to it; if the aircraft arrives overhead on time with horses and jumps still in the arena it's the organisers who will have to pay for the extra flying time involved while they clear the DZ. Medical cover should normally present no problem as the local St. John's Ambulance will probably be out in force, but a small medical pack is a useful part of your own DZ kit. Crowd control is another subject for discussion as quite often it is non-existent at smaller shows and can provide the harassed jumper with another hazard. You should also mention your DZ control and commentary arrangements; most organisers welcome your producing your own commentator but you should check that the latter can see all that is happening from where the microphone is

Photo by courtesy of the Bradford Telegraph & Argus

A display where there ought to have been more crowd control! The author touches down at the Lions Gala, Stanley Park, Blackpool.

located. As part of this discussion you can mention any communications systems you are operating between DZ and aircraft and how they can help in the smooth running of the show.

Sooner or later the show organiser will mention third party insurance and you can tell him of the BPA's policy which covers each individual for third party risks to the sum of £100,000 for any one incident; but if he requires further cover he should be invited to take this out himself. Finally, in company with the organiser, a visit to the local police is good manners and will ensure you of their co-operation at an event where the safety of the public is one of their primary concerns.

The next part of your display preparation concerns the flying side. Ideally you should use the same aircraft and pilot for all your displays as you can build up a smooth operating system which will help you to achieve the best results with minimum fuss. Personally I do not like flying on a display with a pilot I've never met, but perhaps I'm being unnecessarily sensitive. When you engage a pilot for the first time, ensure he's qualified to drop parachutists, that the aircraft is prepared to your satisfaction and that it is equipped with the necessary radio frequencies. The airfield from which you mount the display may not be the aircraft's base and therefore you should check the pilot has fuel and hangarage arranged if necessary. (Remember that landing fees and hangarage fees have to be considered in your original estimate as most airfields charge them.) The nearest Meteorological Office will probably be at the mounting airfield, but you should check on this and have its 'phone number readily available. The difference in altitude between the DZ and the mounting airfield should be ascertained from a map so that altimeters can be adjusted to read the correct altitude above the DZ.

Your next move is to apply to the Civil Aviation Authority for a Special Parachuting Exemption for the display. The only time you do not require this exemption is when the display is given on to a Government or Licensed Airfield, or Approved Drop Zone. The application form is reproduced overleaf and should be completed in every detail and sent to the relevant office of the Civil Aviation Authority (see Chapter 2 for addresses) *at least* 28 days before the date of the display. Attached to this application should be the 6″ to one mile plan of the DZ and written permission from the owners of the land concerned (you may have been able to obtain this at your on-site meeting with the show organisers). If the CAA approve your request they will send you the

Special Exemption, together with any special air traffic instructions that there may be. It must be mentioned that the CAA is always extremely co-operative and any problems can more than likely be sorted out by telephone.

CIVIL AVIATION AUTHORITY
REQUEST FOR PARACHUTING EXEMPTION

Dropping Zone not located at an Aerodrome or notified in Air Pilot.

1. Event...

2. National Grid Reference *1 inch to 1 mile* OS Map of Dropping Zone. (Do not submit map.)
    Sheet No..................Easting.................Northing..............

3. Nearest Town................................... County....................
    Date....................Time(s)........................ (GMT or Local)

4. Map of the Dropping Zone attached.
    Scale 6″ to 1 mile, showing surrounding area indicating buildings, marquees, car parks, spectators' enclosures and any other relevant details, e.g. heights of prominent obstructions and indication of True North. (Scale drawing acceptable.)

5. Height requested...

6. Dimensions of area to be kept completely clear of spectators.........

7. Written confirmation of consultation with local Police at.............
    (This in relation to road traffic control and general public safety for Dropping Zone within $\frac{1}{2}$ mile of an M road or $\frac{1}{4}$ mile of an A road or in built-up areas.)

8. Written permission of the landowner(s). Attached

9. Club or Display Team...

10. Aircraft Type and Registration......Departure Aerodrome.........

11. Signature of applicant................................Date ....
    Name (BLOCK CAPITALS)...
    Address...
                    ....
                    ....
    Tel No(s) (Business hours and alternative).............................

12. Address to which exemption is to be sent (if different from above):
                    ....
                    ....
                    ....

NOTE. This application must be recieved by the Divisional Office concerned, *fully completed*, at least *28 days before the event* to allow for processing, inspection of the site and promulgation of any Air Traffic Notices. The applicant is advised not to begin publicity arrangements until approval has been obtained. *Should the application be incorrect or incomplete it may be returned to applicant for correction or completion.*

The next step may be considered unnecessary but the writing of an instruction for each display is a tidy way of ensuring that everyone knows exactly what is happening. The instruction might well be produced under the following headings which provide a logical layout to cover all aspects:

1. *Demonstration*
   (a) Title
   (b) Day/Date
   (c) Time
   (d) Maps required
   (e) Organisers

2. *Personnel*
   (a) Team Leader
   (b) Team
   (c) Commentator
   (d) DZ Party (to include driver)

3. *Aircraft*
   (a) Type
   (b) Operators
   (c) Aircraft Base
   (d) Mounting Base
   (e) Frequencies

4. *Programme*
   This should give all the timings from when the team meet before the display to the team line-up after it.

5. *DZ Information*
   (a) Brief description to include any particular hazards.
   (b) DZ height and setting of altimeter at mounting airfield.

6. *Communications*
   (a) Details of any radio you may be using.
   (b) All useful telephone numbers:
      (1) Mounting airfield
      (2) Aircraft base
      (3) Showground, etc.

7. *Administration*
   (a) Vehicle
   (b) DZ equipment (to include target panels, smoke flares, anemometer, medical pack, etc.)
   (c) Dress (for team and DZ party).

This instruction should be sent to all the personnel in paragraph 2, the aircraft operators, the show organisers and any relevant air traffic control. The selection of your team is a matter which needs careful consideration. The qualifications are given earlier in this chapter but these can be misleading in that a well trained 'C' Licence holder could easily be more reliable than a happy-go-lucky 'D' Licence holder. Naturally you are going to have to train beginners for displays so start them off on the easier display DZs and have them positioned at the back of any group so that they can follow the more experienced jumpers into the arena. The equipment for the team normally consists of uniform jumpsuits (a well turned out team always creates a better impression than a bunch of scruffs in varying types of jumpsuit), plenty of wind drift indicators and smoke brackets. The latter should be designed with two independent methods of securing them to the parachutist's foot, and team members should be constantly aware of the problems of jumping with smoke and the prime necessity for only setting them off *after* exit from the aircraft. Steerable reserve parachutes are strongly advised for all members of teams regularly jumping into restrictive DZs. (When you next do a display on to a restrictive DZ, have a look at the surrounding area and its hazards from above and ask yourself if you'd be prepared to accept the consequences of cutting away from a malfunctioned main and landing under a non-steerable reserve!) An airphoto or large-scale map of the DZ will assist the jumpmaster in showing exit and opening points to the pilot and members of the team.

The DZ party plays an important part in the display. Apart from being equipped with target panels and medical pack, smoke flares and an anemometer can give the team extra guidance. An anemometer, however, is useless unless it is both accurate and sighted away from buildings etc. where it can give a true reading. The DZ party should ideally be dressed the same as the team and should be carefully briefed on their duties which should include the signals for both temporarily halting the display and for cancelling it altogether should the wind exceed the pre-arranged limits (which may vary depending on the problems of each particular DZ).

A good commentary always adds a final polish to a good display and ideally the team should have its own commentator who knows each individual personally and who can ad-lib with additional details if necessary. A commentator should always be interestingly factual and must resist the temptation to sensationalise the display by saying how incredibly dangerous it is and the like. If you have no regular commentator a commentary brief should be sent to the organisers well in advance together with any photos of the team for publicity before the display.

On the day itself all equipment should be checked before moving off and if possible each member of the team should have a look at the DZ beforehand with its now full car parks and bustling beer tents etc. This is also a good time to set altimeters. After discussion with the organisers and final briefing of the DZ party the team move to the emplaning airfield. Here the team leader can brief the pilot and the team together, having obtained a final meteorological report. The final met. report will give the jumpmaster an idea of whether the team will be reduced by cloud to giving a 'low' show, or if a 'high' show looks possible he will be able to obtain details of the upper winds for calculation of free fall drift. Make sure you emplane and take off in plenty of time.

The exact programme of your display will be dependent upon first, the experience of your team members and secondly, the weather conditions on the day. Initially your displays should be kept as simple as possible and often a simple display, slickly performed, will impress the crowd much more than a shoddily attempted piece of elaborate aerial work. As your team gains experience, your display routine can be developed into a more elaborate affair with, say, cutaways and three or four-man hook-ups, but make sure you have given these routines plenty of practice beforehand.

The display can be cancelled by either the DZ party or the jumpmaster. The DZ party has to make its decision on the anemometer and the jumpmaster's decision will be a combination of his last minute met. check and the distance the streamer drifted. (If the last minute met. check is pessimistic of your chances, it is courtesy to contact the show organisers and, having pointed out the possible outcome, ask them if they want you to fly, bearing in mind that they are paying!) Now a most important point: the decision of the DZ party and/or jumpmaster must NEVER be influenced by either the organisers' pleadings or by the desire not to disappoint the crowd, no matter how many thousand they number.

Once having decided to go, however, each member of the team should know both exit point and opening point. The experienced men should lead the less experienced into the arena but all team members must keep a good look-out around them, especially close to the ground. On landing, just be satisfied on achieving an into-wind landing in the arena, don't be tempted to take a screeching downwind landing on to the cross; it could result in injury (especially on wet grass) and won't impress anyone.

Once your team are all on the ground it will round off the display tidily if you all line up for the crowd. The organisers might well like to take this opportunity to present their president, mayor or similar VIP and this detail is best arranged beforehand.

After your equipment is safely stowed away in your vehicle and you have signed the inevitable autograph or two, you can enjoy whatever hospitality the organisers have laid on for you (assuming you haven't another display to perform). If you can get the pilot along to the post-jump festivities, so much the better.

Finally, when you send the organisers the bill for your display, a covering letter saying thank you for the hospitality or whatever will go a long way towards their engaging you the following year.

Always remember that a well performed display is not only very satisfying but it also benefits the sport as a whole. On the other hand, the press are very quick to pounce on a display that misfires and the subsequent bad publicity can be very damaging. Good planning and strict regard for safety will produce successful results.

Chapter 17

Night Descents, Water Descents and Descents from High Altitude

The three types of descent discussed in this chapter are grouped together because they all tend to be undertaken only very occasionally, being more elaborate in their planning and preparation and thus more expensive. However, they are enjoyable facets of the sport and are satisfactory to have recorded in your log book.

Night Descents

Sport parachuting at night is not purely a question of jumping in reduced visibility but additionally there are the problems resulting from this reduced visibility: the extra equipment needed, the possibility of disorientation, a larger DZ party than usual and the need for a thorough briefing beforehand.

Normally parachuting at night is forbidden by the Civil Aviation Authority and therefore special permission will have to be obtained from the relevant division well in advance. In requesting this permission the Club Chief Instructor should send all details of the programme which should include the names of the parachutists concerned. Parachutists should be at least 'C' Licence holders and the planning and briefing should be undertaken by an instructor well acquainted with the procedures. The planning should include thorough familiarisation with the DZ and its particular hazards, and should be viewed at night to see the location of lights from houses, street lamps etc. The pilot should obviously have a night rating and will be responsible for ensuring that the flying side is organised, i.e. runway and aircraft landing lights, dimmed instrument lights, working navigation lights etc. Apart from an experienced DZ controller less experienced jumpers will be needed on the DZ to ensure that those jumping are reached immediately after landing in case of possible injury.

Extra equipment will be the types of lighting required. Each parachutist should have a torch strapped on the inside of his ripcord-pulling fore-

177

arm pointing towards the hand; its purpose is to enable the jumper to see the reserve if necessary and, once his hands have located the steering toggles, the canopy itself will be lit which will help the DZ party to spot the jumper. Instruments should be lit with a shaded light and this should be red in colour so that night vision isn't impaired. The third personal light is a bright orange or yellow light attached to the top of the jumper's helmet so that he can be readily seen from above both in free fall and under the open canopy. Each of these three lights should be switched on just prior to exit, having been tested on the pre-jump checks. The target should be well lit and in a way that is easily recognisable; five pressure lamps (each manned by a member of the DZ party) set out in the centre of the cross and one on each extremity is as good a way as any.

If there are any prominent hazards on the DZ (e.g. an ADF Aerial) they should also be well illuminated. Normally it is best to throw the wind drift indicator just before last light as a specially illuminated WDI is not always very satisfactory.

The pre-night jump briefing should involve pilot, DZ party and jumpers and should cover the complete routine of each jump emphasising the need for every jumper in each lift to be accounted for before the next takes off. The jumpers should be reminded of the possibility of disorientation (especially on very dark nights), emergency procedures, canopy inspection and the necessity to protect night vision.

The opening point should be clearly marked with a particular pattern of light which might well be two cars with their headlight beams at right angles to one another.

During the descent the jumper should illuminate his canopy as much as possible to enable the DZ party to keep him in sight. Below about 200 feet the jumper should not rely on the altimeter but the odd glance at lights on the DZ will give him a fair idea of his height. The set up for the landing should be facing into wind and relaxed enough to take the unexpected landing. Having touched down safely the jumper should report immediately to the DZ controller to obviate unnecessary searches.

Gradual progression during night descents is imperative and the budding night jumper should not exceed more than ten seconds on his first night descent. Relative work at night is feasible but should be approached with a good deal of caution. In concluding this section on night descents the following four points on night vision are considered most important:

1. Smoking will adversely affect night vision and should not be indulged

in for at least an hour before the descent.

2. Oxygen deficiency adversely affects night vision and starts to take effect soon after take off. This deficiency becomes dangerous above 8,000 feet.
3. Some parachutists naturally have poor night vision and should be dissuaded from parachuting at night.
4. Bright lights adversely affect night vision so beware of bright sunlight that day and photographers' flash bulbs; and the interior of buildings should be avoided for at least thirty minutes prior to take off. Final preparation should be done using red light as this does not affect night vision at all.

Your night jump will only be safely enjoyable if planned in detail; this is also true of the other two sections in this chapter.

Water Descents

Unintentional water descents have already been discussed in Chapter 9 and this section deals with intentional water descents. Intentional water descents provide yet another experience in the sport which is only dangerous when badly planned. As for night descents, water descents should be restricted to 'C' or 'D' Licence holders and the arrangements co-ordinated by an instructor. Normally the Civil Aviation Authority will have to issue a Special Exemption as there are few expanses of water that are located within the boundaries of Government or Licensed airfields. The two golden rules of water descents are first, the provision and use of efficient lifejackets and secondly, the provision of one power boat per parachutist on each stick.

The preparation for the descent consists initially of dress and equipment for the parachutists. The dress is either an old pair of slacks and a shirt, or old jumpsuit, with plimsoles. (If there's the slightest chance of your landing on dry land, a pair of basket-ball boots will provide a little more support.) Helmets are worn as usual. For competition water jumping by properly coached, experienced parachutists a pair of swimming trunks is all that need be worn. The lifejacket is a very important consideration; it should be small enough to be worn under the parachute harness and should ideally be CO_2 operated. Before a water jump in which I participated recently, three CO_2 operated lifejackets exploded during a demonstration of their use; I believe this illustrates the need for the thorough testing of your lifejackets beforehand! You should be aware of the danger of prematurely inflating the lifejacket by accidental operation of the CO_2 bottle either in the aircraft or after exit, as the inflated lifejacket will seriously restrict your movements. If an altimeter is used, some method of preventing its immersion in water must be devised. It is, in fact, possible to carry a large polythene bag and pull it over the whole reserve pack, having unhooked one side after canopy deployment. Preparation in the landing area consists of mooring the target, which may be any brightly coloured inflatable buoy, and the laying on of enough power boats for recovery. The DZ controller must be an experienced parachutist who is well aware of the particular problems involved.

The pre-jump briefing should concern the pilot, the parachutists and, particularly, the DZ party; in water jumping the recovery by boat is probably the most critical feature.

Having exited the aircraft the parachutist will not only be steering his parachute but also preparing for the landing by first undoing the chest strap, secondly sorting out reserve and altimeter as already described, thirdly inflating the lifejacket and finally sitting in the seat strap and undoing the leg straps as described in Chapter 9. It is not a good idea to land directly into wind as there is, in this instance, a chance of the canopy collapsing directly on top of you, which in water has obvious dangers. As you touch the water you can drop clear of your harness and wait to be picked up. If there is any tendency towards your being dragged, you should operate the Capewell release immediately (one of the pioneers of the sport in this country was drowned through being dragged through the water and not having a harness with Capewell releases).

The recovery should go ahead as soon as you touch down with each boat moving towards its own previously nominated parachutist. Two points are worth mentioning: first, the danger of rigging line or canopy fouling the boat's propellor and secondly, once an outboard motor is lifted clear of the water the boat has little or no means of steerage; it would be a pity for the jumper to be run down by the recovery boat!

After jumping into salt water all your equipment must be carefully washed (using a weak soap powder solution) and thoroughly rinsed to avoid the risk of corrosion. Drying both the canopies is simply a matter of hanging them by the apex and allowing them to 'drip dry'; packs and harnesses will take a little longer. Resist the temptation to hang them out in bright sunlight and don't be fooled into believing that the quickest way of drying a canopy is to jump it. This belief came about in an interesting way: a number of years ago extensive tests were carried out at Farnborough using wet parachutes (some of which had been immersed in tanks of water for considerable lengths of time). Each parachute (military static-line type) functioned perfectly. The results of these tests were published out of context in a sport parachute magazine and many sport parachutists believed that the results applied equally well to free fall parachutes. Of course nothing could be further from the truth as a soaked parachute can weigh more than twice its weight dry and so the extractor (or extractors) have double their work load in lifting the sodden canopy and sleeve from the pack tray. Therefore make sure your equipment is dry before you repack.

A well-planned water descent is a refreshing diversion on a warm summer's day.

High Altitude Descents

Parachutists are restricted by the BPA and the Civil Aviation Authority to a maximum jump height of 12,000 feet above the mean sea level without oxygen. Making descents from above 12,000 feet requires a good deal more planning and expensive equipment than water or night descents because of the many problems with which the parachutist is confronted. Any parachutist wishing to make a high altitude descent is obliged to send his proposed plans and details of his equipment to the Safety Committee of the BPA at least four weeks in advance for approval. For this reason I will only outline the problems for I believe that specialised advice is required on equipment and planning which the Safety Committee will be able to arrange. If you are considering a high altitude descent I believe a 'D' Licence should, for your safety's sake be the minimum required.

Lack of oxygen causes a condition known as 'hypoxia' which, if allowed to continue, will ultimately result in unconsciousness. From 10,000 to 15,000 feet the individual tends towards drowsiness and sluggishness; from 15,000 to 20,000 feet drowsiness and sluggishness become more pronounced, thinking is slow and unreliable and vision tends to become blurred. From 20,000 to 25,000 feet loss of muscular control is apparent, corrective and protective actions are not possible and loss of consciousness will follow rapidly. If the individual is exposed to oxygen deficiency his time of *useful* consciousness is reduced with increase in altitude (e.g. he will have thirty minutes of useful consciousness at 18,000 feet, five minutes at 22,000 feet, under a minute at 35,000 feet and no more than six seconds at 65,000 feet). These symptoms of hypoxia will vary with rate of ascent of the aircraft, length of exposure to lack of oxygen, individual physical fitness and tolerance, amount of physical activity and decrease in temperature. To simplify the oxygen requirement it is usual that supplementary oxygen is used in the aircraft until the moment of exit from heights between 12,000 and 20,000 feet; above 20,000 feet oxygen is used both in the aircraft (normally from a console) *and* in free fall (from a bale-out oxygen bottle of about two minutes' duration).

Hyperventilation is another problem with which the high altitude jumper should be acquainted. Breathing involves inhaling life-giving oxygen and exhaling waste carbon dioxide. The provision of additional oxygen at high altitude by rapid breathing (or hyperventilation) simply does not work; instead it produces conditions of dizziness, spots before the eyes and numbness or tingling in fingers and toes which ultimately lead to unconsciousness. If the parachutist experiences these symptoms he may have been hyperventilating and the cure is simply to slow the rate of breathing deliberately or even hold the breath for ten to fifteen seconds; if then the symptoms start to disappear it is a sure bet the jumper has been hyperventilating.

At high altitude cold is extreme, remaining below zero above 20,000 feet the year round. As a rough guide temperature decreases $3\frac{1}{2}°$F for every 1,000 feet; this means that frostbite is another potential problem for the high altitude jumper.

Because of the thinner atmosphere at altitude (above 15,000 feet), terminal velocity is faster (less air resistance to the falling body). Turns and tracking become non-operative above 20,000 feet. The following table gives length of delay (with opening heights of 2,500 feet) above 12,000 feet:

Delay in Seconds	Altitude	Delay in Seconds	Altitude
60	12,500	125	25,000
65	13,500	130	27,000
70	14,500	135	29,000
75	15,500	140	31,000
80	16,500	175	35,000
85	17,500	180	37,000
90	18,500	190	40,000
95	20,000	195	43,500

Because of the problems associated with high altitude jumping I believe that the use of barometric opening devices as an emergency back-up is a sensible idea. It is because of the more costly nature of high altitude descents that they are undertaken least of the three types discussed in this chapter.

Chapter 18

So You want to be an Instructor?

So you want to be an instructor? Fair enough, but why? If it's because you believe that the instructor's rating is the next qualification to be gained in your progression, then forget it! If, however, it's because you feel you have the necessary experience, knowledge and selfless dedication to devote much of your time to teaching and guiding new students in the sport, then read on. Once the student parachutist has left an aircraft on his first descent he is well and truly on his own and his performance will be a direct result of how well he has been instructed *beforehand*. In all other outdoor activities the beginner can work his way up gradually (as in skiing or rock climbing) or he has an instructor actually guiding him (as in flying or gliding). This fact places a heavy burden of responsibility on the sport parachute instructor which he should always bear in mind.

To qualify as a BPA Instructor the following procedure is currently in force:

Potential Instructors

(*a*) Required Qualifications:
    (1) 100 sport parachute descents.
    (2) Two years involved in sport parachuting.
    (3) Category X.
    (4) Club Chief Instructors recommendation.

(*b*) Will be required to attend a one week Potential Instructors Course to be given instruction in:
    (1) Methods of instruction.
    (2) Use of training aids.
    (3) Basic ground training periods such as introduction to equipment, aircraft drills, emergency procedures, and parachute landing falls.
    (4) Practical periods on such as stick inspection, pilot briefing,

student briefing and debriefing, and aircraft drills.

(5) Lectures on such subjects as training progression, safety regulations, etc.

(c)   (1) Will spend six months working under the supervision of one Club Chief Instructor during which time he will be involved in the training of students up to category VIII.

(2) At the end of the six months period, the Club Chief Instructor will be required to write a report and recommendation on the work of the Potential Instructor on an official BPA Report Form.

(d) The Potential Instructor will then be required to carry out a five-day examination period during which time his work (with a normal course of *ab initio* students) would be observed and supervised by the resident Club Chief Instructor of the Centre where the examination is being held. A second examiner (Advanced Instructor) will be present for a minimum of two days observing the work of the Potential Instructor. During this two-day period, a written examination will be indertaken by the Potential Instructor using one of the six test papers (to be reviewed annually) with a minimum pass mark to be achieved. This examination paper would be on such subjects as:

Basic parachute maintenance (recognition of faults, bad assembly and material damage, and contamination).

Student problems/situations.

Aircraft problems/situations.

Documentation.

Displays—Legal requirements, etc.

Basic meteorology.

Basic first aid (fractures, concussion, shock, etc.).

Accidents/Fatalities—Action to be taken.

On satisfactory completion of all three sections, the two examiners will sign the qualification of the Potential Instructor. He will then be qualified to instruct parachutists up to Category VIII standards.

Should the Potential Instructor fail to qualify, he must carry out all three sections again.

(e) The BPA will advise potential candidates of available courses and examination periods.

Advanced Instructors

    (*a*) To be able to instruct all categories of parachutists and instruct in and supervise, competition, night, water and relative work jumping.

    (*b*) Qualifications:

        An Advanced Instructor must be a reliable, mature individual who has the following qualifications:

        (1) Two years as a practising Instructor.

        (2) 500 sport parachute descents.

        (3) D licence qualified.

        (4) Must have done:

            In intentional water jump.

            A night free fall descent.

            An intentional cutaway jump.

    (*c*) Method of Qualification:

        A potential Advanced Instructor must submit proof of the above qualifications during a personal appearance before the Safety and Training Committee. The Safety and Training Committee will decide, by a vote, whether the person should be accepted as an Advanced Instructor.

    (*d*) Examiners:

        The Panel of Examiners will be selected from the more experienced Advanced Instructors by the Safety and Training Committee.

    (*e*) Both ratings are to be renewed every two years.

        To maintain an Instructor Rating, an Instructor must have a recommendation from his Club Chief Instructor which will state that he has been engaged in student training regularly during the previous two years and that he is suitable for renewal.

        Advanced Instructor Ratings will be reviewed over two years by the Safety and Training Committee.

This procedure is straightforward enough but in itself gives little idea of the type of person who will make a good instructor. This is of singular importance as a really good parachutist does not necessarily make a good instructor and, vice versa, a good instructor need not be an outstanding performer himself. When compiling the BPA Parachuting Regulations in 1967, General Dare Wilson gave his ideas on the qualities of a Sport Parachute Instructor. These qualities I quote with the addition of a few extra thoughts of my own which I consider important:

1. The type of parachuting with which we are concerned is that which people do for enjoyment. That is why it is called sport parachuting, and the good instructor must realise this and do as little as possible to interfere with the enjoyment of the sport. He must therefore be *approachable*. (There is a tendency amongst instructors to become less approachable with their gaining more expertise and a position of more stature within their club; this tendency towards aloofness should be strongly resisted, as any student should feel completely at ease to approach his instructor with any query, however trivial it may seem. It is also worth the instructor casting his mind back to his own student days and remembering the difficulties with which he himself was faced; humility is part of approachability.)

2. The primary concern in all parachuting must always be safety. It almost goes without saying, but not quite, that the good instructor must be *safety-conscious*. (In an effort to beat the prevalent poor weather record in this country to get the student a jump, the less experienced instructor may be tempted to bend the rules: DON'T! Any sport parachuting decision could almost always be made correctly having asked yourself the question 'Is it safe?')

3. Safety cannot be achieved without supervision and a willingness on the part of all concerned to stick to the rules which is, of course, discipline. In order to produce discipline an instructor must be *firm*. (He will almost always find it easier to be firm if he is also fair; in a student's natural enthusiasm to progress quickly he will appreciate the instructor's firm decision to do another static line descent before going on to free fall (for example) if the reason for making him do it is explained fairly.)

4. The good instructor, who is responsible for the safety of those in his care, should therefore be firm, but not overbearing. He must accept only the response and compliance under which safe parachuting can be conducted. He will, as in most other activities, achieve much by *good example*. (The average student will always regard his instructor with a certain amount of awe and will inevitably tend to follow his example whether good or bad, or whether connected with parachuting itself or not. It is important that the student parachutist sees his instructor doing plenty of parachuting himself or he will tend to say to himself something like 'There must be something magic about this sport if

my instructor doesn't participate'. I personally believe that the instructor (or instructors) should jump on the first and last lift of each day.)

5. Free fall parachuting is more than a skill. It requires a cool head, concentration and judgement, as well as body control and agility. In the early stages a novice is liable to feel a little apprehensive. The instructor can help him to overcome this by imparting *confidence*. There is only one thing worse in this respect than a lack of confidence, and that is over-confidence. The latter leads to acceptance of risks which in turn inevitably result in accidents. An over-confident parachutist is a menace to himself and to others; he should be supervised closely and if necessary suspended.

6. Parachuting can be a complex matter, and the supervision of it more so. The instructor carries a great deal of responsibility and has much to think about. He cannot, for example, instruct others if his mind is on his own parachuting. When he is instructing he must concentrate wholly on his instruction. In order to ensure that nothing is overlooked, he must by *systematic*.

7. When conditions are right for parachuting there is a tendency for people to become impatient. Haste leads to danger, because sooner or later something important is overlooked. 'If you are in a hurry, you are in danger' is a good parachuting motto. The good instructor must therefore be *alert but unhurried*.

8. Parachuting is not always straightforward. Many parachutists experience problems sooner or later. Most of them are minor, but at the time they are cause for concern. Often the parachutist cannot determine the reasons for his problems and it is up to the instructor to spot them for him and explain how they can be overcome. For this reason he must be *observant*. (There is a good deal of skill in being able to spot the student's mistakes and then deliver a clear critique to him afterwards. It is a skill which develops with practice but its importance cannot be stressed enough for the student is wasting his jump if he is not learning from it.)

9. There is no substitute for practical experience. The highly experienced is better than the less experienced because he has personally met and overcome many of the problems which from time to time will confront his pupils. But no instructor, however expert, will ever experience all the problems of others. He will, however, often be called upon to give advice, and in order to do so he must understand parachuting in all its aspects, and this can only be achieved through intensive study and

intelligent discussions. To this end he must have an *enquiring mind*.
10. Only a limited proportion of capable parachutists make good instructors. They often lack one or more of the qualities referred to above. Even if they have them all, there is yet another as important as any of the others. In accepting his responsibilities a parachute instructor is entrusted with the lives of others. This he must never for a second forget. He must never take a chance or run a risk, however small, in case the outside chance comes up. In order to avoid the acceptance of risks he must in the first place recognise them as such, and in order to achieve the standard of knowledge which this demands, he must be dedicated to his responsibilities. Until, therefore, he has a sound knowledge of all aspects of the sport coupled with considerable practical experience and ability to instruct, he should not put himself forward as an instructor, let alone be considered in this connection by the Panel of Examiners.

BPA Parachuting Regulations, 1967 are a must for the would-be instructor and can be obtained on application from the BPA Office. On your road to being granted an instructor's rating, your qualification as a Ground Instructor will give you additional responsibility and will help you gain experience and knowledge which will undoubtedly benefit you in your ultimate examination by the two members of the BPA Panel of Examiners. A Ground Instructor may be appointed only by Club Chief Instructors in order to assist with ground training and organising duties. Rules governing Ground Instructors are as follows:

(*a*) They must be over 21 years of age.

(*b*) Notification of their names, and particulars including their BPA numbers must be notified to the BPA *before* they assume their duties.

(*c*) Their duties will be confined to the ground unless they are also qualified to act as Jumpmasters. They may include the following:
(1) Supervision of parachute packing.
(2) Parachute fitting.
(3) Ground Training Instruction.
(4) Marshalling.
(5) DZ Control.

(*d*) Ground Instructors are responsible only to the CCI of the Club who submits their names to the BPA. They will have no authority to instruct at other Clubs or Centres unless additional registration is undertaken with the BPA.

(e) Ground Instructors will be selected with particular regard to their experience, reliability, attitude towards safety and ability to inspire confidence. They should be well established and respected within a Club before they are appointed.

Two of the duties of a Ground Instructor require more explanation. The first of these is parachute fitting, which is the preliminary to the actual pre-jump inspection, or 'pin check' as it is commonly called (originating from the vital check of the ripcord pins). Every parachutist, no matter what his standard, should be checked before emplaning and therefore the following check list should become second nature to all parachutists of General Permit standard and above:

Front View

Main Parachute and Harness
1. Capewell releases – turn sideways to ensure correct assembly.
2. Capewells level and at correct height.
3. Ripcord handle seated firmly in pocket.
4. Ripcord leading freely into housing.
5. Ripcord housing not floating and unobstructed (three inches maximum).
6. Breaststrap correctly buckled.
7. Legstraps correctly buckled.
8. D Rings correctly attached to harness.
9. Loose ends of harness tucked away.

Reserve Parachute
10. Ripcord handle seated firmly in pocket and unobstructed for immediate use.
11. Ripcord pins fully inserted through cones. (Check for bent pins and presence of sand or grit which could interfere with opening, especially on back mounted reserves.)
12. Pack opening bands correctly hooked up and NOT obstructing ripcord.
13. Pack correctly hooked on to D Rings by serviceable snap connectors.
14. Tie-downs securely buckled to back-pack and under tension.

Instruments

15. Stopwatch wound, set for use and in working order if to be used.
16. Altimeter(s) adjusted and at least one 'non-sensitive'.
17. Instruments correctly seated.

Personal Dress

18. Helmet fitted with reliable strap fastening system (NO peaks).
19. Boots of a suitable pattern.
20. Gloves of a suitable pattern (obligatory in cold weather), and especially suitable for operation of reserve.
21. Goggles (if worn) of suitable design.
22. Overalls well fitting and fastened up. All loose objects secure.

Smoke Generators

23. Securely attached to boots by two independent attachments, with pins firmly seated so that they cannot work loose of their own accord.

Back View

Back Pack

24. Corner flaps tucked in.
25. Ripcord housing secured to pack and unobstructed. Metal plate must NOT be bent.
26. Ripcord leading freely into housing on main (and reserve if latter is back-mounted).
27. All pack opening bands present and correctly hooked up.
28. Pack stiffeners not broken or bent.
29. Ripcord pins correctly seated in cones.

The second important duty of a Ground Instructor may well be that of DZ Controller. The exact duties will be produced by the Club Chief Instructor in writing and mounted on a board for easy reference. The following is a comprehensive list of the recommended duties of a DZ Controller:

1. He will be responsible for setting up and supervising the DZ Control Organisation as required by the CCI.
2. He will be given clear instructions from the CCI on the extent, if any, to which he is responsible for the briefing and supervision of marshallers, Jumpmasters and parachutists.
3. He must ensure that pilots briefing includes any DZ Control Instructions or information which are of concern to them.
4. He will brief any assistants or staff who are placed at his disposal or who are in any way made responsible to him by the CCI.

5. He must lay out the target at the point indicated by the CCI.
6. He must display the appropriate ground-to-air signals for the guidance of pilot and Jumpmaster.
7. He must set up and maintain watch on a wind system, or be in constant communication with someone who holds this responsibility.
8. He must ensure that an ambulance or stretcher-carrying vehicle with First Aid Kit is at all times immediately ready to attend to casualties. The driver or another nominated member of the ground staff must be trained in First Aid, and one or other of them should know the quickest route to the nearest hospital.
9. He must ensure that the target area is clear of parked vehicles and other hazards.
10. He must prevent large groups of spectators from approaching too close to the target area.
11. He will maintain a close look out for aircraft including gliders, and will suspend parachuting as soon as any interference with the safe conduct of parachuting becomes apparent.
12. He will keep a close watch on wind and weather and suspend parachuting if either should exceed or threaten to exceed the limits laid down.
13. He will ensure that all apparatus for wind indication on the DZ is put to proper use and the attention of the CCI drawn to any equipment which is lacking or unserviceable (wind socks, signal panels, smoke generators etc.).
14. He will keep in close touch with Flying Control, if there is one adjacent to the DZ.
15. He will maintain radio communication with the parachuting aircraft if it is provided.
16. He must personally observe all parachute descents, preferably through telemeter or binoculars until all parachutists have landed.
17. He will ensure that all landed parachutists who are in need of assistance receive it without delay.
18. He will report all accidents, injuries, parachute malfunctions and contraventions of BPA Safety Regulations and Club Rules to the CCI.

Having gained your instructor's rating you may well find yourself as the sole instructor in your club; if this is the case you will automatically assume the position of Club Chief Instructor and the responsibilities that go with it. Chapter 4 gives the ten basic rules for the conduct and control of sport parachuting and I shall now discuss some of your additional responsibilities as a CCI.

When a person approaches you expressing his desire to become a sport parachutist you must initially satisfy yourself of his suitability to undergo parachute training and the reasons which lie behind his ambition; the following two paragraphs are quoted verbatim from BPA Regulations, Part 1:

> There are many reasons why people wish to parachute and not all of them sound or laudable. Bravado, the desire to impress others, the result of a wager or a dare and even a tendency to suicide have all been encountered. One of the more common of these reasons is the secret desire to prove certain characteristics to themselves which they suspect, often with some justification, they do not possess. The mental conflict which ensues in the mind of the pupil is better avoided if an instructor can detect his true motives for wishing to parachute.

> "Instructors should interview all candidates and try to assess their reasons for parachuting. Those who do not appear to be suitable in any way should be politely but firmly discouraged. It is quite wrong for any parachutist to adopt the attitude that 'anyone can jump if they put their mind to it'. The fact is that only a minority of able-bodied people do make parachutists for many sound and obvious reasons. There is no point in encouraging anyone to take up sport parachuting if they are likely to injure themselves or are unlikely to enjoy it."

This responsibility for accepting students for training is a heavy one and it is experience which will ultimately enable you to decide whether to accept someone or not.

Another problem will arise sooner or later and that is the one of refusal to jump. It is an interesting one in that it is often the unexpected person who refuses and the obviously nervous one who doesn't, but whenever it happens you should be fully conversant with the procedures. The student will announce his intention to refuse at any time after take-off, but usually on the 'jump run' itself. He may either tell you he isn't going to jump or freeze where he is or move out on to the strut and then freeze. If it's one of the first two alternatives you should tell the pilot to go around again and then talk to the student, telling him that he's got another chance. If he's on the strut you may be able to coax him back into the aircraft; if not, his fingers will slowly come unstuck and he'll drop away; (virtually all refusals are static line students so this eventuality is OK!) If, once you have talked to him, he is still adamant about not jumping, you should move him to the back of the aircraft, dispatch the other students and then ride down with him. You should talk to him on the way down in an effort to restore his now bewildered ego. Once on the ground you should enter his refusal in his log book, date it and sign it. It is up to you whether you let him have another chance, but personally I don't for the following reasons: first, his refusal will have an upsetting effect on the other students in the aircraft; secondly, he has shown that he is far from being 'switched on'; thirdly, he will probably ask to have another go only in an effort to redeem his self-respect, and finally, in the majority of cases, once a student has refused he will do so again and again (if given the chance). If you are forced into advising him to take up another sport then this is just another one of your more difficult jobs.

Another of your responsibilities as a CCI is the thankless one of ensuring that all documentation is up to date. You should first ensure that each club member's personal documents are up to date, and the easiest way to do this is to have an individual record card for each member, listing his documents and their validation. Secondly, you should ensure that you keep a record card for each parachute (main and reserve); this card should detail all packings, repairs and modifications. Finally, you should keep a daily record of all parachute descents to include: date, aircraft, pilot's name, names of parachutists, heights and details of any injuries or malfunctions. Actually it is best to record malfunctions in a separate book which should give complete details and any recommendations or action taken to prevent its recurrence. At the end of each year the BPA will call for an annual parachuting return to include details of number of descents, injuries and malfunctions. Do you still want to be an instructor?!

You are also responsible for passing out pilots to drop parachutists. Before doing so you must ensure that the pilot concerned has one hundred hours 'in command' flying and is thoroughly familiar with the type of aircraft to be used; this being satisfactory, he should be briefed on exactly what is expected of him (this has been covered in Chapters 5 and 13). You should then go up with him and have him fly for a live drop (the aircraft may be filled up with 'C' Certificate Holders). Having satisfied yourself of his performance you can now recommend to the BPA that he is qualified to drop parachutists. This recommendation should include his CPL or PPL number, his total hours 'in command' and his approximate number of hours on the main types of aircraft he has flown. Having been checked out in this way, the pilot is then responsible for the loading of the aircraft and all other relevant details in connection with its use for parachuting.

Static Line Procedure

Static line procedure requires a section of its own in this chapter for, as an instructor, much of your training of students will depend on its correct use. I shall discuss the use of the static line from packing to dispatching and you will see that its correct use is both logical and safe. The static line itself should be twelve to fifteen feet long, made of nylon or cotton webbing of at least 3,000 lbs breaking strain. It should have a small loop in one end and ideally the American Sliding Clip at the other (recently carabiners with screw locks have been introduced and have proved a safe substitute). The static line as a whole should be checked for serviceability before use. As the stage in packing of closing the pack itself is reached, the loop at the end of the static line should be attached to the loop at the base of the extractor using a piece of 50lb cord. The pack is then closed in the normal way with two exceptions: first the ripcord does *not* pass through the housing and secondly, a piece of 50lb cord (about 4″ long) is placed through each hole in each cone before inserting the ripcord pins. The static line comes out of the pack between the third and fourth pins from the top, a small loop is made and it is then laid alongside the pins. Each length of 50lb cord is then tied tightly around each pin and *not* around the ripcord cable itself. The remainder of the static line is now neatly 'S' folded and stowed in two elastic bands which are in turn attached to two small webbing loops sewn on the tops of each side flap of the pack. The practice of attaching the elastic bands to the two top pack opening bands is not recommended. The static line clip can be temporarily hooked on to the chest strap 'D' Ring. The pack opening bands are now done up in the normal way; beware of the horror of hooking up the left hand pack opening bands to hooks sewn on the outside of the ripcord protector flap–the pack simply cannot open in this condition. The ripcord protector flap is left open and the ripcord handle stowed temporarily under the top right hand pack opening band. (See Figure 28.)

The student is now ready to put on the main parachute in the normal way. Before the chest strap is done up, the static line clip is unhooked,

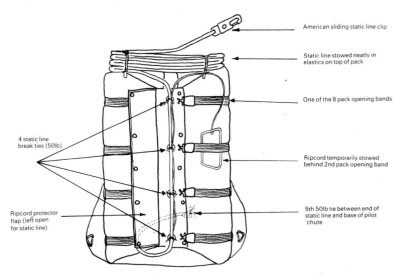

American sliding static line clip

Static line stowed neatly in elastics on top of pack

One of the 8 pack opening bands

4 static line break ties (50lb)

Ripcord temporarily stowed behind 2nd pack opening band

Ripcord protector flap (left open for static line)

5th 50lb tie between end of static line and base of pilot 'chute

Fig. 28. Main pack rigged for static line use and ready for pre-jump checks.
1. Remove main ripcord handle.
2. Check each break tie.
3. Check pack opening bands.
4. Check static line stowage.

left open and given to the student to hold in whichever hand is suitable for the exit he is to use. The stick now line up for the pre-jump checks. It is at this stage that the instructor carefully removes the ripcord (bearing in mind that as a result, tension is applied to the break-ties themselves). The stowage of the static line is checked, followed by an individual check of each break-tie. The rest of the pre-jump check is as normal and the student is then ready to emplane after the pre-jump briefing. (A word of caution here: if the reserve tie-down is tightened too much, extra pressure will be put on the break-ties which could cause them to break).

The instructor himself should also be prepared with the following additional pieces of equipment: a copy of the flight manifest mounted on a clip board, with a biro (for recording critiques of the students' performances), a sharp knife and a carabiner (with screw lock) attached to one of the reserve 'D' Rings (we will examine their use shortly).

At 1,000 feet the static line clip is taken from the student's hand and he is hooked up as necessary. (The number you hook up at this stage will depend on the size of the aircraft and whether it is equipped with an overhead cable.) At the same time as the student is hooked up, a further individual check is made of each break-tie. After hooking up, the student himself should be allowed a tug at the static line to reassure himself of its attachment to the strong point. At the beginning of the run-in the student should, if possible, adopt a kneeling position facing the door and the instructor should ensure that static line is running free from the strong point to the top of the pack. The spot should allow the student time to move into the door, being guided by the instructor who is taking the static line in his hand nearest the door. The student, having positioned himself for exit, should look in at the instructor who in turn will shout 'GO!', simultaneously tapping the student's knee with his other hand. The instructor's hand which is gripping the static line should be held against the top rear corner of the door frame, as it is this hand that takes the tension as the five ties break during deployment; in fact the static line is only secured to the strong point as a safety precaution. This control of the static line by the instructor is very important and will be covered in great detail during his apprenticeship; if the instructor at any time loses control of the static line it could result in a malfunction or worse still – a hang-up.

Once the student has left the aircraft the instructor must not take his eyes off him until after full canopy deployment. Being able to spot a student's every little mistake comes with experience but his performance must be carefully noted and recorded in biro on the flight manifest in the remarks column as soon as it is convenient. The static line should now be pulled in, unless the aircraft has an overhead cable, in which case it may be left outside until the last static line student in that stick has jumped. If the aircraft is then going to climb higher for the more experienced jumpers it is most important that the static lines are un-hooked from the strong point and stowed carefully out of the way – to be suspended under the aircraft by a foot tangled in a hooked up static line is likely to be very unfunny!

Now what of the hang-up drill? The case of the conscious student has been discussed in Chapter 7; the unconscious student is a little more tricky, however. If this situation should arise the pilot should be instructed to fly over a clear area and, if possible, gain height. The instructor should check his knife and hook his carabiner (still attached to the reserve 'D' Ring) around the static line. Now the instructor eases himself out of the door and slides gently down the static line, the cara-biner allowing him use of both hands. Once he reaches the student he should take hold of the reserve ripcord handle in one hand and cut through the static line with the knife in the other. As soon as both student and instructor fall free, the latter pulls the reserve ripcord handle before pulling his own a second later. I grant you that the hang-up, in either form, is a highly unlikely event but you must be absolutely sure in your own mind how you will tackle it should it occur.

Once on the ground the debrief of the student is of prime importance with each moment of the jump being carefully examined. The debriefing is probably best done collectively with each individual coming out in front of the remainder to learn of his mistakes or otherwise; in this way students may learn from each other's performance. Remember that as an instructor the progression of the student is entirely in your hands and his natural enthusiasm may well make him try to persuade you to allow him a faster progression; you're the boss and you must make the decision in the interest of the student's safety.

Conclusion

Training sport parachutists is very hard work but it can be very satisfying, especially if the instructor takes a genuine pride in teaching and guiding his students. Experience will improve an instructor's technique and ultimately he may consider himself fit to qualify as a BPA Advanced Instructor.

There are very few really good instructors who are devoted to the time-consuming task of student parachute training. Do you really think you could be one of them?

The suspended harness is a valuble training aid

APPENDIX A

SECTION I – CONDUCT AND CONTROL

1. Overall responsibility for ensuring that the ten BPA Basic Safety Rules (see Chapter 4) are observed within Affiliated Clubs, Schools and Centres rests with Club Chief Instructors (CCIs). A lone instructor automatically assumes the responsibilities of a CCI.

2. Student parachutists will only parachute under the organised control of a BPA Affiliated Club, School or Centre and under the supervision of a CCI or BPA Instructor authorised by a CCI.

3. 'C' Certificate Holders parachuting in groups will only do so when the most experienced amongst them has assumed overall responsibility.

4. 'C' Certificate Holders parachuting independently will only do so in accordance with BPA Regulations.

5. All Clubs, Schools and Centres will establish a satisfactory system of Ground Control to control parachuting.

6. All parachutists must be briefed before emplaning and inspected.

7. All aircraft lifts must be correctly manifested before take-off.

8. DZ Control must be continuously established when parachuting is in progress.

9. The descent of all parachutists must be observed from the ground.

10. Parachutists under instruction must be debriefed after every descent.

11. Parachutists' log books and other relevant records must be kept up to date.

12. The DZ Controller must be a BPA Instructor or Ground Instructor.

13. DZ Controllers must be positioned so that they can observe the landings of all parachutists on the DZ.

14. The DZ Controller's duties will be recorded in writing, signed and dated by the CCI.

15. Club and personal records of descents and parachute packings must be made in the appropriate log books, registers and record cards the same day as they are made.

16. An Instructor or Ground Instructor must be nominated by the CCI to take charge of the packing area.

17. All parachutes must be checked for damage after every descent and withdrawn from use if found unserviceable.

18. The packing of parachutes by parachutists without packing

certificates must be adequately supervised and checked at the appropriate stages by a member of the Ground Control Staff nominated by the CCI or Instructor in charge of the packing area.
19. All Clubs, Schools, Centres and Display Teams will use the BPA system of Ground to Air Signals.
20. Every DZ must be equipped with a windsock or other means of indicating the strength and direction of the wind to parachutists in the air.

SECTION II – INSTRUCTORS
21. CCIs will be responsible for the safe conduct of all parachuting activities within their Clubs etc., and for the maintenance of Club parachutes and safety equipment.
22. CCIs may ground any parachutists using their DZs for violating BPA or Club Safety Regulations.
23. All BPA Instructors must have their instructors rating renewed at least every two years.
24. All BPA Instructors must be qualified as laid down in Chapter 18. All are duty-bound to correct and report breaches of safety.
25. Ground Instructors are responsible only to the CCI of the Club, who submits their names to the BPA; they have no other authority to give any instruction or supervision except that called for by their CCI.

SECTION III – JUMPMASTERS
26. No aircraft with more than one parachutist aboard will take off without a Jumpmaster being appointed.
27. Jumpmasters will normally be the most experienced instructor or parachutist on board an aircraft.
28. Jumpmasters must brief the pilot and all parachutists in their lift before emplaning.
29. Jumpmasters are responsible for inspecting all student parachutists in their lift immediately before emplaning and ensuring that 'C' Certificate Holders have inspected each other.
30. In an emergency Jumpmasters will seek and follow the instructions of the pilot, who is in command of the aircraft and all parachutists on board.

SECTION IV – EXAMINERS
31. A BPA Examiner must not recommend the appointment of an Instructor if there is any doubt in his mind concerning the candidate's suitability.

SECTION V – CLASSIFICATION OF PARACHUTISTS
32. Parachutists must not be recommended by the CCI for a 'C' Certificate before they have been classified as Category VIII Parachutists.

SECTION VI – PILOTS
33. Pilots must be examined and recommended for parachute dropping in accordance with the procedure laid down in Chapter 18.

SECTION VII – AIRCRAFT
34. Only aircraft approved by the Civil Aviation Authority and cleared for parachuting by the A and AEE Boscombe Down may be used for the dropping of Sport Parachutists.
35. All aircraft used for dropping parachutists must be suitably prepared.

SECTION VIII – EQUIPMENT
36. The equipment to be used by sport parachutists must be in accordance with the requirements outlined in Chapter 3.
37. 'C' Certificate Holders are wholly responsible for the safe condition of their own equipment and for ensuring that checks and inspections are carried out on it as required.
38. CCIs are responsible for the maintenance and safe condition of all items of Club equipment, and for the serviceability of any personal equipment used by student parachutists under their supervision.
39. All BPA Clubs, Schools and Centres must have a satisfactory system of documentation covering all parachutes and property. It must provide for the recording of all packings, repairs and modifications.
40. Parachutes will only be modified by those technically qualified to do so.
41. Parachute modifications must be carried out in accordance with BPA policy and only by those authorised by CCIs or the BPA Safety and Training Committee.
42. All parachutes must be packed according to a system approved by the manufacturer.
43. Clubs are responsible for training their pupils to pack parachutes and for giving the necessary supervision until they are given a Packing Certificate.
44. Parachutes will not be stored in a damp condition. Silk parachutes

will not be repacked or used in a damp condition. All parachutes which have been immersed in sea water will be thoroughly cleansed with fresh water before drying or packing.

45. When a parachute has been packed for ninety days or more it may not be used before it has been unpacked, aired and repacked.

46. Parachutes which are not fit in every respect for immediate use will NEVER be packed with the appearance of a serviceable parachute. They should be closed with the sleeved canopy clearly showing at each end of the pack, the ends of which should be open to view.

47. At least a single altimeter must be carried on all parachute descents involving a planned delayed opening of fifteen seconds or more. Instruments must be securely mounted in such a way that they do not interfere with the operation of the reserve parachute.

48. At least one non-sensitive altimeter must be included among the instruments carried.

49. All parachutists must submit personal Automatic Opening Devices to their CCI for inspection before taking them into use.

50. All parachutists must be clothed and equipped according to the requirements outlined in Chapter 3.

51. Smoke Generators may only be carried by 'C' Certificate Holders and with the permission of their CCI.

52. No wings, cloth extensions or any other form of additional control surfaces may be used as part of the dress or equipment of any parachutist.

53. Static line operation must be according to the BPA approved system unless the permission of the BPA Safety Committee is granted for the use of an alternative system.

54. Twin extractors when used will both be attached to a single bridle cord.

SECTION IX – MEDICAL

55. All parachutists must have a valid medical certificate as outlined in Chapter 2.

56. CCIs will be guided by the advice contained in Chapter 18 when accepting applicants for instruction.

57. No parachutist may take any form of alcoholic drink before he has completed parachuting for the day.

58. Parachutists must not drink heavily during the evening before parachuting the following day.

59. Parachutists who do not feel fit in all respects, and particularly if they have a head cold, must not parachute until they have fully recovered.

SECTION X – TRAINING

60. Parachutists who do not progress or respond satisfactorily to training must be suspended by their CCI.

61. Clubs must maintain records showing what training has been completed in the case of every individual. They should include details of any problems encountered and the response of the student to corrective instruction.

62. Ground training as outlined in Chapter 4 must be given to all novices.

63. The pattern of training of all parachutists must follow the BPA System of Parachutist Classification given in Chapter 11. This rate of progress, which reflects that of an above-average parachutist, should in no circumstances be accelerated.

64. Emphasis in training will be given at all stages to the importance of the correct use of the reserve parachute, and the need to handle reserve parachutes in aircraft with the greatest of care.

65. All parachutists will be instructed to follow the drills laid down for use after landing.

66. No student parachutist will complete more than three parachute descents in a day. Following three full days' parachuting student parachutists must be given one complete day of rest from parachuting.

67. The greatest care will be taken in the use of small aircraft for the training of parachutists.

68. Student parachutists who have not made a descent for two months or more will revert to the static line or short delay before being allowed to progress.

69. 'C' Certificate Holders who have had a lay off of six months or more will resume parachuting with a delayed drop not exceeding ten seconds.

70. No parachutist will use a 'TU' or comparable advanced canopy until he has qualified as a Category V parachutist.

71. No parachutist will be permitted to use a 'Paracommander' or similar high performance canopy until he has qualified as a Category VIII parachutist (see Chapter 7).

SECTION XI – WEATHER

72. Ground wind limits for parachutists are as follows:

(a) Category I–V Parachutists	4·5 metres per sec.
	10 m.p.h.
	9 knots
	14 feet per sec.
(b) Category VI–IX Parachutists	6·5 metres per sec.
	15 m.p.h.
	13 knots
	22 feet per sec.
(c) Category X Parachutists	8 metres per sec.
	18 m.p.h.
	16 knots
	26 feet per sec.

These limits will under no circumstances be exceeded.

73. Every Club must use an anemometer for measuring ground wind speed.

74. Suspension of parachuting will be ordered for the categories of parachutists concerned after TWO gusts above the limit have taken place within FIVE minutes. After parachuting has been suspended it will not be resumed for at least thirty minutes during which no gusts above the limit have occurred.

75. The strength and direction of winds below 2,200 feet AGL will be measured by the use of Wind Drift Indicators (WDIs).

SECTION XII – WIND MEASUREMENT

76. WDIs will be used in accordance with the instructions contained in Chapters 8 and 13.

SECTION XIII – DROPPING ZONES

77. All DZs with the exception of Government and Licensed airfields must be approved by the Civil Aviation Authority. The information they require is contained in Chapter 16.

78. DZs will be selected in accordance with the standards given in Chapter 16.

79. Where open water, excluding minor rivers and small ponds, exists within 1500 yards of the target all parachutists must wear inflatable life belts or carry life preservers ready for immediate use.

80. No DZ will be used for routine parachuting which has High

Voltage Power Lines running within 1000 yards of the target, and if less than 1500 yards all parachutists will be briefed from an aerial photograph.

SECTION XIV – PARACHUTING LIMITATIONS
81.   Sport parachuting at night is prohibited by the Civil Aviation Authority without special permission.
82.   Parachutists will not intentionally drop or be dropped through cloud.
83.   All static line descents will be from 2,500 feet AGL.
84.   'Jump and Pulls' will not be made below 2,200 feet AGL.
85.   In all delayed opening descents canopies must be opened by 2,000 feet AGL, except 'D' Certificate Holders taking part in displays who may delay their opening so that their canopies have opened by 1,500 feet AGL.
86.   No parachuting will take place from above 12,000 feet ASL without Oxygen.
87.   Clubs and Members who wish to parachute above 12,000 feet ASL using Oxygen must submit their plans and details of their equipment to the BPA Safety and Training Committee at least four weeks beforehand.
88.   Deliberate water jumps may only be made in accordance with the instructions contained in Chapter 17.
89.   No one under the age of 16 may make a sport parachute descent.
90.   Minors of 16 may only parachute with their parents' or guardians' written consent.

SECTION XV – SAFETY IN THE AIRCRAFT
91.   No person will approach a moving aircraft.
92.   There will be no movement in the vicinity of an aircraft forward of the wings.
93.   The Jumpmaster is responsible to the pilot for the safety of all parachutists in the aircraft. The pilot is in overall command.
94.   The Jumpmaster is responsible for the orderly emplanement of his lift and for their supervision and instruction as necessary in the aircraft. All parachutists are under his command until they leave the aircraft.
95.   All parachutists must fit their helmets before take-off and fasten safety belts if provided.
96.   The dropping of the WDI and subsequent spotting must be carried out, or supervised, by the Jumpmaster.

SECTION XVI – SAFETY DURING FREE FALL
97. Not more than four static line parachutists may be dropped on any one run over the DZ.
98. In delayed opening descents from 3,000 feet AGL or below, not more than one student parachutist may be dropped for every 150 yards of DZ.
99. When a parachutist loses control in free fall and is unable to regain it he must operate his main parachute immediately, regardless of whether he is above the normal opening height. Such cases must subsequently be investigated by CCIs.
100. In free fall the lower man always has the right of way over the higher man.
101. Relative parachuting must be carried out in accordance with details given in Chapter 15.
102. The use of cameras in free fall will be confined to Category X parachutists. Club Members must submit their equipment to their CCI for inspection.

SECTION XVII – SAFETY DURING PARACHUTE DESCENTS
103. Parachutists will keep well separated from each other after opening their parachutes. At all times they must give way to those below them.
104. All student parachutists must land into wind until such times as their CCI allows them to do otherwise.
105. Student parachutists will not attempt stand-up or competition landings.

SECTION XVIII – EMERGENCY PROCEDURES
106. No parachutist will leave an aircraft in emergency without obtaining the pilot's permission. If communication with the pilot is not possible the Jumpmaster must take command of the parachutists on board and use his own judgement.
107. When flying over the sea parachutists must wear inflatable life-jackets or carry life preservers ready for immediate use.
108. Adequate fire fighting appliances must be available on all airstrips from which parachuting aircraft are operating.
109. In the event of a parachute opening inside an aircraft in flight, or of a 'hang-up', the Jumpmaster will follow the procedures outlined in Chapters 5 and 18.

110. All Jumpmasters must carry a knife in an aircraft for use in emergency.

SECTION XIX – MALFUNCTIONS

111. The only type of approved temporary packing pin is a ripcord complete with handle or a series of pins attached to each other and distinguishable by a red tag.

112. All malfunctions must be noted in a special register and any parachute which is suspect must be immediately withdrawn from use for expert examination.

113. Parachutists who are prone to malfunctions and related problems must be given special attention by their CCIs. If the latter think it advisable they must be suspended in their own interests. Such cases must be reported to the BPA.

SECTION XX – PARACHUTING ACCIDENTS

114. Non-fatal accidents, other than normal landing injuries, must be fully investigated by Clubs and reports submitted to the BPA as soon as possible.

115. Fatal accidents will be investigated by the BPA except when Servicemen on duty or parachuting on Ministry of Defence property are concerned.

SECTION XXI – PARACHUTING DISPLAYS

116. Parachuting Displays must be given strictly in accordance with the details given in Chapter 16.

SECTION XXII – COMPETITIONS

117. Student parachutists and those with fewer than fifty free fall descents will not be permitted to enter any Parachute Competition.

SECTION XXIII – PERSONAL DOCUMENTS

118. Personal documents must be maintained, checked and renewed as laid down in Chapter 2.

SECTION XXIV – CLUB RECORDS

119. Club Records must be fully and accurately maintained.

SECTION XXV – REPORTS
120. Clubs, Schools and Centres are required by the BPA to submit an annual parachuting return, and Malfunction and Accident reports as necessary.

APPENDIX B

BIBLIOGRAPHY
By no means a complete list, the following books and magazines are, however, a fair coverage of the sport.
Books
1. Alone in the Sky – Mike Reilly – Robert Hale 1963
   The first English book on sport parachuting by one of the country's pioneer sport parachutists, it includes a history of parachuting, why's and wherefore's and personal reminiscences; a little dated but worth reading.
2. Birdman   – Leo Valentine – Hutchinson 1955
   An autobiography by the great French pioneer who discovered that man could 'fly' without wings.
3. Skydiving   – Bud Sellick – Prentice Hall 1961
4. The Space Age Sport – Ray Derby – 1965
5. Parachuting for Sport – Jim Greenwood – Modern Aircraft Series – 1962
   These three books (all American) start with a history of the sport and go on to the why's and wherefore's – not comprehensive but worth reading.
6. Sport Parachuting – Russ Gunby – Herald Printers 1969
   A very comprehensive American handbook which is a most useful addition to the parachutist's library.
7. Panic Takes Time   ⎫
8. Parachuting & Skydiving ⎬ – Dumbo Willans
   Partly autobiographical and partly factual,

these two readable books are by the 'Father of English Sport Parachuting'.

8. Falling Free — Cathy Williamson – Robert Hale 1965
Largely autobiographical, this book tells the story of the 1964 Australian Ladies' Team Captain's participation in the sport.

10. The Falcon's Disciples – Howard Gregory – Pageant 1968
Subtitled 'Parachuting's Unforgettable Jumps' it contains an escapist selection of the raciest jump stories. Great fun.

11. Skies Call — Andy Keech–1974
A photographic essay on sport parachuting of outstanding beauty. All colour.

Magazines

1. Sport Parachutist — The official magazine of the British Parachute Association,
Kimberly House,
47 Vaughan Way,
Leicester LE1 4SG.

2. Parachutist — The official magazine of the United States Parachute Association,
P.O. Box 109, Monterey,
California 93940.

3. Spotter Magazine — An American magazine of considerable variety
109 Park Street,
Dorchester,
Massachusetts 02122, USA.

4. Les Hommes Volant — The official French parachute magazine — excellent if you speak French!
28 rue de Navarin,
Paris (9e).

5. Australian Skydiver Magazine — Billed 'Skydiving as the Aussies see it'.
Post Office Box 9, Kensington Park,
South Australia 5068.